Children's Domestic Work

Children speak out for themselves

Children's Domestic Work

Children speak out for themselves

Vinod Chandra

MANAK
PUBLICATIONS PVT. LTD

First Edition 2008

Published by

MANAK

PUBLICATIONS PVT. LTD

B-7, Saraswati Complex, Subhash Chowk,
Laxmi Nagar, New Delhi 110092
Phone: 22453894, 22042529
E-mail : manak_publications@hotmail.com
manak.publications@gmail.com

ISBN 978-81-7831-168-5

Layout by
KHUSHNUMA

Laser Typeset by
T. ALI
Hamdard Nagar, New Delhi

Printed in India by
Nice Printing Press, New Delhi

This book is dedicated

to

My mentor and spiritual guru

Late Shri Sushil Kumar Sharma

CONTENTS

PREFACE

Research on domestic work suggests that if mothers spend more hours in paid or unpaid work outside the home then fathers' contribution to household chores increases. This does not mean that the reduced household work of mothers due to their paid jobs is completely shifted to fathers. Children in such families share much of their mothers' work. Research on children's domestic work has shown that in dual earner families the share of domestic work of children increases significantly. Lee and others (2003) very aptly raised some unanswered questions about children's domestic work. They talk about the relationship of domestic work and personal competence and self-Esteem of children; the relationship between domestic work and educational achievement; the relationship between the domestic work and Children's sense of responsibility; and the role of children's domestic work in the professional and occupational achievements of parents. Even my own quest was to know the role of children's domestic work in the maintenance of the social order of the family. To understand children's domestic work there are two main dimensions. First is to assess the impact of children's housework on family's domestic economy. How family receives it? There are plenty of studies in US and Europe where scholars outlined the role of children's contribution to domestic work for the maintenance of the economics of the family. However, the second dimension of the study of children's domestic work is to examine its impact on children themselves. The developmental psychologist and child sociologists tried to explore this dimension cursorily. In the whole range of scholarship, what I found that children's own experience of their domestic work through which they undertake different household chores in challenging situations was missing. To fill this gap in understanding of children's housework and to answer some of the pertinent questions raised by many scholars in the past I found my study of children's work in the family settings in Britain which I undertook for doctorate degree at the University of Warwick as an important ground material. The present book is a modest attempt to deal the basic questions on children's housework.

This book offers a careful examination of existing research on children's domestic work and refers to recent sociological studies showing the changing trend in the concept of children and childhood. The value of children's domestic work has been changing over the years in the literature of both developing and industrialised countries with the acknowledgment of children's actorship and the need for a new perspective — the child perspective. Chapters II and III together explain this background. Chapter III states the theoretical development justifying the new approach. The socialization theory leads to the development of a sociology of childhood and validates the need for the new approach in future research on children. The signs of change, and the research conducted on this basis indicated in chapter two and three, together serve as pointers to the course adopted in the present study. Methodological issues are also outlined in chapter IV that give the reasons for adopting a qualitative method which suits the problems posed by the theme as well as providing a reasonable direction for the investigation in view of the aim of the study. The children's perspective advocated earlier is adopted as the most expedient approach.

Chapter V explores empirically whether the activities of children in the family account to 'work' by referring to various types of activities — self-provisioning, house maintenance and caring — in addition to examining their extent. It concludes that child's contribution to domestic work and domestic economy as work is above board. The argument that children are contributors to domestic work in contrast to the view that they create work for others, is reinforced through exploration of the extent and nature of their work in chapter V. Their experience helps in understanding domestic activities as work. The same experience is analysed in chapter VI to find out its sociological implications. The meanings domestic work has in different contexts for children, and its significance for them and the family, are probed in this chapter. Domestic work is seen as a tool in their hands, which affects both their childhood and the social order of the family. The subtle role of gender and age as structural factors in the experiences of children's domestic work warrants a detailed examination of their influence. This carried out in a separate chapter in this book. To understand children's lives in their social and economic context it is noted that gender and age are not sufficient considerations: attention to their interaction is imperative. This is specifically done in chapter VII. Gender and agency are found not only to limit domestic work but also to motivate children to find ways and means to vent agency. When gender and age interact this provides a good opportunity for children to utilize their capacity to negotiate. The immanence of agency through the constraints of gender and age has enabled children to re-construct their childhood and refined their social relationships. How the concept of seniority in the consideration of age plays a unique part in Indian families is revealed in this chapter.

Chapter VIII concludes in the form of argument developed through out the book. The findings and conclusions are discussed along with their implications. In sum, it is argued that children's experience goes to show that their contribution to domestic work and domestic economy stands out and is substantial and children in both Coventry and Lucknow demonstrate that, although the socio-economic and cultural context do play a part in their contribution, they express the force of agency in constructing and reconstructing their childhood and defining and refining social relationship. It follows that children's work has a social significance. It does not merely have a narrow developmental value in the personal context of the child, which has mostly been the view so far. Some issues – both important and ancillary — for further research which could not be addressed in this study are also pointed out.

15 March 2008 Vinod Chandra
J N Post Graduate College
Lucknow

ACKNOWLEDGMENTS

I owe my thanks to a great many people whose help has played a crucial part in the completion of this book. First and foremost, my warmest thanks are extended to the children who admitted me to their lives and shared their experiences so generously. They are integral to the study which I have reported in this book. Without their active participation and unstinting help this study may never have completed. I only hope that I have done the experiences they have shared with me and the information they entrusted to me the justice that it deserves.

It is my pleasure to gratefully acknowledge the constant intellectual inspiration, critical advice, and over all good cheer that I received from Prof Christopher J Pole, Dean, School of Social Science, Nottingham Trent University, UK and Dr. Philip J Mizen, Reader in the Department of Sociology, University of Warwick, UK who have not only supervised me during my PhD degree at the University of Warwick but keep guiding me till today in all my research activities. Their intellectual stimulation, constructive academic advice and most valued of all their friendship contributed significantly to my research and understanding on children from more than one decade.

I owe a debt of gratitude to those have helped me in a

variety of ways in this study. In particular, Prof Eleanor Nesbitt had read and commented on my work at various stages. I interacted with Prof. Muhammad Anwar, Prof. Robin Cohen and Dr. Parita Mukta for understanding issues related to ethnic minorities in Britain during my stay in Coventry. I I pay my sincere thanks to all of them for their practical help and moral support. I have discussed parts of this research at the World Congress of Sociology held at Brisbane in 2002 and at Durban in 2006, International Conference on 'Childhoods 2005' held at Oslo in 2005. I am grateful to all those who commented on the presentations and helped me to shape the present monograph. I have also benefited from the discussions with Dr Virginia Morrow whom we call Ginny and Prof Olga Nieuwenhuys on many occasions in the past. I wish to pay my sincere regards to Prof Berry Mayall who was the examiner of my thesis. Her encouraging comments on my monograph motivated me to bring it in the form of a book.

The Commonwealth Academic Staff Scholarship provided me the best possible support during the course of research for PhD degree at the University of Warwick, UK for which I am indeed grateful to the Commonwealth Commission. I am also thankful to the University Grants Commission, New Delhi, the University of Lucknow, and Sri Jai Narain Post Graduate College for supporting me for this study by granting me study leave for four years.

I pay deepest gratitude to my parents and in-laws for their constant support to all my academic endeavour. It is their blessings and sacrifices which have enabled me to pursue the privileges of this study. In particular, I express my deep gratitude to late Shri Sushil Kumar Sharma, my true *guru* in all respect, for his belief in my abilities which has been a source of great strength. I have no words to express my feelings for his support from the very beginning for this work. This book would have not been completed without the support and unstinting help provided by my everlasting friend and caring wife, Aparna. She not only helped me in reading the manuscript at different stages, but made me laugh when things went wrong. She stayed with me every step of the way. She deserves my sincere thanks. The cooperation of my daughter Shambhavi and my son Vatsal has been incalculable. This book would not have appeared without the support given by Shri M P Yadav Publisher of Manak Publications. So, I thank to Shri Yadav and his team for bringing out this book in record time.

Aurhor

1

INTRODUCTION

Reconsidering Children's Work

Sociology of Children's work has been slow to develop. Where children figured in sociological analysis, this tended to be restricted to the sociology of family and the sociology of education, but in both an examination of the social meaning of their work finds no place. Even in the sociology of work, children have failed to feature to any significant degree. In fact the definition of work which has for a long time prevailed in discussion of the sociology of work is not self-contained and comprehensive enough. It addresses only those activities as 'work' which is performed by adults and found to be productive. This definition of work ceased to conceptualize 'work' in 'essentialist terms' (James *et. al.*, 1998:102). The omission of various unpaid tasks (e.g. household tasks, self-provisioning activities, gardening, etc.), which are directly or indirectly responsible for the conditions of production or reproduction of economy, has come under severe criticism (Morris 1990, Pahl 1984). Feminist Scholars, in particular, have stressed the need to expand notions of work to include unpaid work (e.g. housework, caring etc.) in the sociological definition of work. To some extent the domestic labour debate has succeeded in securing the acknowledgement of women's unpaid housework in the wider division of labour. Nevertheless, children's unpaid housework has been left out altogether in the domestic labour debate. However, children perform numerous unpaid tasks which contribute to both the productivity and the income of the family and which at the same time make it possible for a member of the family to augment the family income e.g. the tasks which, if not done by children, would entail a cost to the family.

More importantly, the conventional concept of work regards it as the province of adults. Work is usually discussed in relation to the concept of adulthood, whiles the concept of childhood traditionally belongs to the realms of development and socialization (James *et. al.*, 1998). When children's work is studied it tends to be examined within the parameters of development and socialization. The work in children's life tends to appear as an apprenticeship or as work-experience and preparation for their future life. As a consequence, the social meaning of work in children's life has been largely obscured or restricted to notions of 'child labour'.

The invisibility of the social meaning of children's work is inextricably linked to the concept of the child. What is considered as 'the child' has a direct bearing on the understanding of children's work. Historically, the concept of 'the child' in the West has gradually developed during the nineteenth and twentieth century (Aries 1962). The social constructionist view explains how children became progressively separated from adult social world, particularly in the area of 'work' and 'labour' (Aries 1962; Archer 1995) as legislative provisions were introduced to prohibit children from working in factories during this period. The compulsory education system on a national level placed children in schools (Fyfe 1989; Weiner 1991). Thus participation in formal waged work was removed from children's lives that were progressively excluded from the production process. After retrieval from the labour market children were placed either in school or the family which were considered as areas of 'free' from the exertions of work. Their activities in the family and school were regarded as beneficial for their development. The exclusion of children from the world of productive work resulted in development of an image of children as unproductive and, therefore, dependent upon others for their well-being. This image further placed great emphasis on children's biological immaturity, irresponsibility and incompetence and childhood was considered as a period of transformation from the stage of 'becoming' to full social 'being'. Treating children in terms of their future and not the present effectively renders them as a deficient social group. In this approach, children's work was seen as an index of developmental processes and further underlined the invisibility of work to children's lives (James and Prout 1997). That is why Mizen *et. al.*, have aptly commented that children's work is seen "primarily as a marker of adolescent development or as pre-figurative episode in their socialization into normative patterns of working life" (1999: 426). Consequently, considerations of the meanings of work for children themselves have been largely excluded from debate.

In general terms, children's paid employment is generally seen to have undesirable implications for their development and hence it is usually regarded as, at best problematic and at worst unsuitable. Children's work in the factories is termed unsuitable on the grounds of its hazardous nature and unhealthy conditions, and philanthropist organizations and labour movements tend to designate it as 'child labour' necessitating abolition. "Much of the attempt to map and quantify children's work comes from agencies intent on its reduction, control or elemination" (James *et. al.*, 1998:123). The international agencies such as the International Labour Organization (ILO) and UNICEF campaign against abusive and exploitative forms of child labour and have developed a distinction between suitable and unsuitable work for children. In common usage the term 'child work' has been used for suitable and acceptable forms of work, while the term 'child labour' denotes exploitative and unsuitable forms of work. For example Fyfe holds that "Clearly not all work is bad for children. This view commands almost universal agreement. There is little doubt that many children welcome the opportunity to work, seeing in it the rite of passage to adulthood and a positive element in the child's development. Light work, properly structured and phased, is not child labour. Work which does not detract from the other essential activities for children, namely leisure, play and education, is not child labor. Child labour is work which impairs the health and development" (1989:4)

Similarly, Whitakar (1986) observes that economic compulsion drives children into 'child labour' whereas children's help in household chores or delivering newspapers are suitable. On the distinction between suitable and exploitative work of children, Lavalette (1996) notes the situation in Britain is that "children continued to undertake work tasks but from the turn of the twentieth century they have been identified with a particular type of employment, part-time out of school work, performed before or after school, at weekends or during school holidays. These jobs are not normally identified as exploitative child labour but as 'light work tasks', particularly suitable for children. Thus they are more commonly perceived to be invigorating and healthy past times which children carry out for a little extra pocket money." (1996:175)

The policy driven distinction of 'child work' and 'child labour' developed by international agencies is fundamentally clouded by political and moral considerations (James *et. al.*, 1998, Nieuwenhuys 1994). It does not map the whole picture. The suitable forms of children's work have been subsumed under the process of socialization and only unsuitable forms of children's work have been discussed in debates about children's work. Child labour as an immoral and exploitative activity thus represents only a small element of the work that children do. The distinction between child labour and child work appears to promote the healthy development of children but the writings on child labour, at times, fail to make out even a clear distinction between the diverse forms of labour, let alone children's work (James and others, 1998). Children's activities are not co-extensive with morality; they lie much beyond it.

This incomplete picture of children's work has come out because of the dominance of the adult's perspectives. The full circumstances of children's work have not been understood. Children's own views and experiences have not been considered as a means of understanding their work. The adult-centric child-development view precludes children's work in its full context. This situation has prevailed in the research on children's work for a long time. Theoretically and empirically it has contributed to a failure to understand the full extent of work to children's lives. However, the recent rethinking of children and their childhood offers the opportunity to throw a new light on the issue of children's work. In these debates children have been considered as *social* beings in all senses and children have been reconceptualised as a permanent structure of every society (Corsaro, 1997). Furthermore, accepting the children as social actors in their own rights suggests the need to place them in the division of labour in society. Thus Qvortrup (1985) argues "that children's objective position in the social division of labour would justify, on theoretical grounds, the child group being assigned a distinct status or class. Children take part in socially necessary activities, contribute towards the accumulation of knowledge and labour power to be used in society, are permanently a part of social renewal, and from early age are in integral part of social organization" (1985:141-2).

The concern with children's position in society received a further impetus through the UN Convention of the Rights of the Child (CRC) in 1989. The CRC represented a further challenge to the traditional way of looking children solely in terms of their potential as future citizens. It posed a challenge to the 'conceptual pair of socialization and development' (James and Prout, 1997: ix). One of the key recommendations of the CRC is to recognize and ensure children's participation in the wider society. The CRC's perspective emphasized certain rights for the child (as that of adults) in society. Within this approach the child as a person in his/her own right has been legitimized. The understanding of children's work only from the vantage point of the developmental perspective also received qualification. Pettitt maintains that "there has been a move to look at children as active social and economic participants — as workers rather than as passive consumers" (1998:2). What is glossed over by the earlier approach is now recalled for reconsideration. To place it in perspective, a reconsideration of children's work requires two simultaneous efforts. The first is to recognize the renewed concept of child and childhood and respect their competencies as workers; and the second is to take into account the purlieus of work — i.e. activities akin and close to the concept of work and examine their content as well as meaning for children and others.

Given the recognized need for studies to focus on the meanings of work, including the meaning for children themselves, this study explores the significance of children's work within the boundaries of the household. In this context, the children of Indian families, who run their retail businesses shops, are most appropriate for the study for two reasons. Firstly, the existing research on small-scale ethnic businesses in Britain informs us that along with the ethnic shop owners their spouses are heavily engaged in pooling of labour in the business (Srinivasan 1995, Basi and Johnson 1996). This certainly creates a good opportunity for examining how children contribute to domestic work. Secondly, these families also offer an opportunity for children to contribute to family businesses too, which existing research suggests is another important element of family life (Song 1996).

Locating children's domestic work in the debate

Children's work in the family has remained marginalised both in the debate about the division of domestic labour and in the debate about child-labour. Commenting on this lacuna Corsaro (1997) argues that whenever children do figure in the debate on domestic labour it is striking that they have been seen only as the object of additional labour. .Feminist authors, Delphy and Leonard (1992), have recently realised that one of the major limitations of the debate on domestic labour is that it ignores the contribution of men and children. When we try to look into the reason for the prolonged exclusion of children from the domestic labour debate we find that the feminist movement gained currency during the 1970s and 1980s, when feminists were concerned mainly with women's position. The issue of domestic labour was concerned only with the role of women in the family and children were marginalised. In addition to this, the prevailing notion of children positioned them as both dependent and incompetent. This socially constructed image thus excluded the possibility that children are competent contributors to domestic work. These two factors contributed to the non-recognition of children's work in the family.

The child labour debate does appear to offer an area where children's work in the family should find a place. However, as referred to above, it so happens that under the concept of acceptable forms of activity it has been subsumed under the developmental framework. Using this framework to understand children's work is itself highly contentious. It is based upon a particularly narrow view of work according to which child work could not be recognized within the family atmosphere since it is here that children are considered completely under the protection of parents (James and others, 1998). This assumption has been challenged by a number of researchers (e.g. Light *et. al.*, 1985, Taylor, 1973). They argue that it is not always true that children's work within the family under the supervision of parents is essentially beneficial. Light and others (1985) found that the majority of the children of migrant workers in the United States (i.e. 68% of their total sample) were substantially contributing to both domestic work and farm work. Their work was found to be arduous.

The emphasis on the distinction between 'acceptable' and 'unacceptable' forms of work further marginalizes the importance of the social and economic values of children's work.

However, in the recent past the attempt has been made to highlight the importance of children's work for others too. It has been shown that children's work in the family affects all the people who live around them and who relate to them in any way. For example Mayall (1996) has shown that children's activities affect the social order of the family, while Solberg (1990) has found that children's household activities can affect parents' working life. Morrow (1992) has demonstrated how children's domestic work contributes to the domestic economy. Children's school activities have also been shown as work which affects others (James and Prout 1997). The findings of recent research give a further impetus to recognizing a diverse range of children's activities as work that is socially meaningful (James *et. al.*, 1998).

In sum, both the domestic labour debate and the child labour debate have marginalised children's contribution to family work for different reasons. It is to the credit of recent research that child labour has been increasingly recognized but it is noteworthy that this has dealt with only specific points in relation to children's work in the family. There has been no research which has examined children's domestic work after discussing and defining 'work' crisply so as to make out a justifiable case for children's work in the division of labour in the wider society and so as to vindicate its social and economic meaning.

Towards a definition of children's domestic work

As noted above, children's domestic work is largely ignored in the debate. Recently developed sociological research on children's work, however, unearthed the multiple contexts and motives which suggest a broader horizon of children's activities, particularly in relation to the division of labour. Solberg's (1990) attempt to explain the social implications of children's work for the negotiation of age and its meaning; Morrow's (1994) account of children's work within their families or in the educational system to explain children's economic role in labour market and in their household; Song's (1996) research on children's 'helping out'work in Chinese take-away businesses; and James and Prout's (1997b) attempt to explain children's school activities as work all point out a far more extended area of children's productive work than is traditionally acknowledged. Emphasising a reconsideration of the scope of children's work, James *et. al.*, (1998) have suggested that the scope of the definition of work should be widened. They suggest that this reassessment should not only include an idea of which activities should be classified as 'work' but, also how their context and motivation change and how children understand them. It should also try to find out how children's involvement in work affects and is affected by their social relationships and how children's work "is involved in the construction of children's lives as a whole" (1998:120). With this object in view an operational definition of work will be suggested to include all activities of children which affect their and others lives in some way in the family. It will encompass activities like caring for themselves and for siblings and others, cooking, house maintenance, laundry, gardening, shopping, and taking part in family business, etc.

The importance of children's perspective: The speaker without a platform

Until recently little attention has been given to children's own experience of work particularly in the construction of their own social and economic life. Children own perspective on their work has been largely invisible in analysis since most studies of children's work rely on information offered by parents. Wherever children have been included in the research process it is remarkable that they have been asked only to report on what work they do and the conditions under which they perform these tasks. Their experiences and views have not been engaged in exploring the social meaning they attach to their work. In such studies the role of children has been that of an informant only. They are not heard on their work and they are not allowed to appear as meaning-makers. Thus, others (who are either parents or researchers) made the judgments about the value of their work.

Some recent studies have taken note of children's perspectives while examining children's work. During the investigation of children's work, Save the Children (1998), for example, has examined not only the reasons why children work but also what they think about it; how they are treated at work; and how work fits into their lives. This approach brings out several new factors concerning work. For example, the reasons for working include responsibility, gaining independence from parents, gaining parental respect and establishing relationships with others. In this way, the stereotyped reasons for gaining money either for themselves or for the family are left far behind. The question of what the children thought about work also received interesting replies. The children tended to see work as playing an important role in their lives and it also gave them a degree of satisfaction. However, elements of work were found to be stressful and problematic at times. Their description of treatment meted out to them at work also demonstrates how fundamental this point is to experience. Apart from discrimination on the grounds of sex they were also given the worst jobs. They were not even listened to and were often ill treated by parents on the plea of protection. They were aware of economic exploitation of themselves. In short, the study found that work played a key part in children's lives. In addition to this, while studying work of Danish children Frederiksen (1998) disclosed several reasons for working apart from money. Indeed adult assumptions about the working life of children and youth may not be the only valuable and insightful approach. This observation, which confirms the views of Petitite above, underlines the importance of children's perspective.

Woodhead (1998) has also commented that children's work experience alone can elucidate the positive and negative effect of work on them, their personal vulnerability, its causes and its contexts, the value placed on their activities and ultimately how they are or can be seen as social actors. Listening to children's feelings, views and perceptions is an essential source of evidence on the way work affects them. Morrow (1994) arrives at an interesting point in understanding why children work and finds that their work roles articulate those of adults as well as mirror adult's work. She realises the need to move away from the socialization view that children are pure dependents and, therefore, primarily a burden on the family. In another article in 1996 Morrow argues that far from merely being a burden on their families some children may be making an important contribution to household labour through the routine of daily tasks and child care they undertake. The concept of dependency in her view masked children's capability, competency, agency and responsibility. Her study in fact, paved the way for a fuller explanation to the children's views of work. Julia Brannen (1995) has pinpointed the main reason for ignoring children's contribution to household work. It is on account of the absence of a child's perspective in sociology. Of the recent studies which have taken note of children's perspective Solberg's (1990) has a special significance as it deals with their contribution to the family's economy — fishing— and family work in the absence of parents. It makes out a strong case for attitudinal change by taking children's perspective in the research of children's work. In an attempt to theorize childhood, James *et. al.*, (1998) have noted that the view of the child has not been appropriately considered in studies on their work. They therefore suggest that research should now take into account children's perspective in considering how work takes places in their life and how it is made socially meaningful. It is not only necessary to give greater attention to their own account but also essential to regard with respect their ability to take decisions about their lives. Boyden *et. al.*, (1998) also strongly suggest that children's work should be empirically investigated through their own perspective.

Research conducted on issues related to children on other areas than work also underpins the importance of children's perspective. The issues of health (Mayall 1996), religion (Nesbitt 1999) and schooling (Prout 1997) in children's lives have been addressed through children's perspective and added a new dimension to the understanding of children's social worlds. The scope of religion's embrace is considered as a powerful reason by Nesbitt (1999) for wishing to understand children's perspectives on religion. So is the case with children's work in the family which spans a vast area of work in the present study. It includes domestic work as well as work related to family shops. The concept of many 'childhoods' leads to the understanding that work have different meanings in different situations. What meaning a work has and for whom is an important consideration in this context. An outsider cannot derive the meaning which work has for the worker himself. It is, therefore, in this sense that the experience of work among children counts when we want to know its meaning and significance. This study deals with the work of children in different social settings — Coventry and Lucknow. This inevitably warrants children's views and their interpretation of work done by them. Children's perspective is therefore of key importance and ideally one of the multiple perspectives (parents' perspective, employer's perspective) required to determine the ambit and impact of work on children. At the present juncture it is not merely a complementary perspective but a perspective that is all-important as it rectifies and counter balances the view on their work provided by others.

2

CHILDREN'S DOMESTIC ACTIVITIES: Work or no Work?

Children's work in the family is an under-researched subject. The last few decades have seen a plethora of research produced on children's work in the developing world. However, this research primarily focuses on the hazardous and exploitative forms of paid employment. Much of children's work is left out in this research as it is neither exploitative nor harmful. This has happened partly because the research was basically founded on the definition of work set by international agencies. For example, the International Labour Organisation (ILO) defines work as an economic activity which emphasises only paid activities (Boyden *et. al.*, 1998). Children's paid labour is seen to be more vulnerable to exploitation. The nature of work, the conditions of work, and the motivations for work are considered as main criteria for exploitation. These criteria vary from region to region and from context to context. A type of work may be exploitative for children in one regional context while the same is beneficial in another. Given this difficulty, the wide range of children's work such as farm work, housework and work in an artisan's family has largely been left out of the discussions. Those kinds of work which are done under parental supervision have also been ignored as they are seen as their training for the future. It is also believed that there is no or only very little scope for the exploitation of children in such work.

By contrast, exploitative forms of child labour in western countries are usually seen as the problem of the past. As such they have rarely been the subject of research. Although some efforts have been made to rediscover the problem of child labour in the western world in the recent past, research has mainly concentrated on children's paid work just as it has in the developing countries (e.g. MacLennan *et. al.,* 1985; Light *et. al.,* 1985; Greenberger and Steinberg 1986; Hobbs and Mckechnie 1997; Lavalette *et. al.,* 1995; O'Donnell and White 1998; Mizen 1997). In this way, children's unpaid work particularly *within* and *for* the family has largely been ignored in both parts of the world. This is so because the generally accepted concept of the child did not allow children to work productively and, therefore, wherever they have been found to be working their work was either condemned or explained as beneficial to their development and a part of their socialization process. Within this conceptualization, children are supposedly trained in the family under the best supervision of parents who are deemed agents of socialization. This led to a situation where there is little reason for scholars to suspect that children contribute to domestic work and have a productive role in the family.

However, there are a number of studies on children in western countries which have dealt with the issue of children's domestic activities (Straus 1962; Thrall 1978; White and Brinkerhoff 1981; Goldscheider and Waite 1991; Benin and Edwards 1990, Manke *et. al.,* 1994, Gill 1998). Although the focus of these studies was to understand children's domestic activities, this was only as a part of their socialization. These studies have examined related issues such as the extent and nature of children's involvement in housework, their motivations to housework, the impact of their housework on their development and factors affecting their involvement in housework.

The Main Issues Related to Children's Work in the Family

The nature and extent of children's work in the family

The existing literature on children's activities in the family reveals that children undertake household tasks in both developing and western countries. For example, children of the developing countries undertake various types of work in and for the family, ranging from work in the house to work on family farms. Particularly in peasants economies boys work in the fields; they help in farming during the peak season of the harvest; and girls do domestic chores such as cooking, cleaning, fetching water and fuel, and caring (Cain 1977, 1982; Caldwell *et. al.*, 1984; Mamdani 1981). These children substantially contribute to both productive work and social re-productive work within the families (Maharatna 1997). For example Maharatna's study of peasant families in Orissa (India) finds that during the harvest season children, particularly girls, were found to be involved in domestic activities for long hours as their work "presumably provides support, enabling adult members to devote longer hours to directly productive work" (1997:367). Kanitkar's (1996) study of 200 girls (from both rural and urban areas) reveals that more than 90 percent of the girls were involved in regular domestic chores which include cooking, cleaning vessels, sweeping, stitching, care of siblings, minor repairs and shopping for everyday household items. Reynolds's anthropological study of children's work in the subsistence agriculture of the Tonga people of Zimbabwe reveals that children contribute 57 percent of their family's productive work including domestic work. These families might not be able to meet the labour demands of farming without children's contribution.

These studies have also explored the extent of children's work and find that they spend a considerable number of hours on domestic work. For example, Maharatna's study finds that boys and girls devote 2.33 hours and 3.59 hours per day respectively to domestic work. In another study, Bhattacharjee finds that "in rural India a girl works for nine hours and, on an average, for 315 days in a year in the fields and at home. By the time she ceases to be a child (i.e., 14 years), she has provided economic help to the family worth Rs. 39,600" (1985:2). A study undertaken by the Indian Institute of Science, Bangalore, shows that a girl child spends 29 per cent of her total time on gathering fuel wood and 20 per cent on fetching water. Nieuwenhuy's study in Poomkara (Kerala, India) finds that children "rise at 6.00 a.m. and only lay down as late as 10.00 p.m. which leaves them with eleven hours to devote to work in and around the house" (1994:73). Her study finds that girls spend the major part of the day in assisting their mother in household chores. It is also interesting to note that these children begin to contribute to housework from a very young age. For instance, Dube (1988) notes that in the household of fishermen of coastal Andhra Pradesh (India) boys of the age of 12 started accompanying their father fishing and girls aged 10 started cooking with their mothers, while five-year olds started collecting firewood.

In some cases the extent of children's involvement is so heavy that they have to drop out of their schools (Nieuwenhuys 1994, Das1988). In her study Nieuwenhuys (1994) finds that some girls have given up their schooling because of the excessive load of domestic chores. Das's study also reports the similar findings that "some girls do join school but most leave soon after. Nishtha started a school with 45 students, of whom 25 were girls. After six months, there were only four girls left. The girls were so busy with household chores that they had no time to come to school. They had to look after siblings, collect firewood, organise food for domestic animals, fetch water, etc." (1988:33).

Due to their responsibilities for housework children have to compromise on school, play or leisure. This situation is acute in developing countries as reported above but there is some evidence in western countries too, which show that children have to lose their school and entertainment at the cost of their family responsibility. Morrow (1996) reports that in her study of Cambridgeshire children there are a few instances where girls disclosed that they have to drop their school for a day or so because of the increased household responsibilities at the time of contingencies.

Studies in western societies too have noticed the extent and nature of children's housework (White and Brinkerhoff 1981, Goldscheider and Waite 1991, Manke *et. al.*, 1994). White and Brinkerhoff's (1981) study of 790 Nebraska (America) families explores the actual extent and nature of children's housework. Children of these families were found to be contributing substantially to housework. They undertake tasks ranging from self-care to house maintenance. This study shows that children of the age of ten and above help their parents in various domestic chores. In some situations these children not only help but also replace their parents by undertaking their jobs.

In another study Goldscheider and Waite (1991) finds that children share almost 15 percent of household tasks according to their mothers. Mothers in American families reported, according to the study, that out of seven frequently shared tasks, washing dishes and cleaning the house are the tasks which children do with a good deal of responsibility. The study reports that children undertake mainly cooking, cleaning, laundry, child care, dishes, yard work and grocery shopping. Since the information on children's share in household tasks is gathered only from mothers, possibly under-estimates their involvement. Despite this qualification the study recognizes the three cornered division of domestic labour—i.e. mother, father and children.

The extent of children's share in domestic work in western families is measured in time-use studies too (Benin and Edwards 1990; Mauldin and Meeks 1990; Manke *et. al.*, 1994). For example, Benin and Edwards compare the time spends by children in domestic work in full-time dual earner families and part-time dual earner families. They find that in full-time dual earner families, daughters spent 7.5 hours per week in excess of boys while in part-time dual earner families both boys and girls spent 2.5 hours per week on domestic chores. Manke *et. al.*, (1994) study compared children's work in single earner and dual earner families. They have also found that children of dual earner families contribute substantially to domestic chores. British studies also indicate findings similar to those as of the American studies. For example, Morrow's (1992) study reports that children's contribution to household tasks is substantial. These children undertake a wide range of tasks in the family. A Norwegian study (Solberg 1990) also produced similar findings.

Studies in both developing countries and western countries shed a new light on children's contribution to domestic work. Whatever be the focus of these studies, at least this research has clearly shown that children's work in the family is not such that it can only be seen in terms of their training of future roles.

Explanations for children's work in the family

Children's involvement in domestic work has been explained mainly by demographic, economic, socialization (child development), and anthropological perspectives. The demographic perspective chiefly explains the causes of children's involvement in peasant economies. Scholars who share this perspective were interested in explaining the population growth in developing countries. They have paid attention to fertility behaviour, the demand for children and the need for birth control. They have expounded the utility of children for peasant households and documented children's contribution to their economy (Hull, 1975; White 1975, 1976; White and Peet 1978). High fertility was traced to a wider socio-economic environment in which parents hoped that their children would contribute to the domestic economy (Cain 1977; White 1976; Nadkarni 1976; Mamdani 1972, 1981; Fawcett 1978). It is argued that the children's availability for domestic chores and farm work in peasants' families is the major motivation for a high birth rate (Schultz 1973; Fawcett 1972; Caldwell 1976; Wong 1977). For example, Mamdani's research on Indian peasant families notes that these families need a large number of working children to achieve their ends as children were found to contribute substantially to both domestic work and farm work. However, Maharatna (1997) finds that, besides the children's value as a source of labour in peasant families, there are some other considerations for having a large number of children. For example, he finds that socio-cultural obligations and old age security for parents are equally important considerations which play a decisive role in the greater number of children per family. Moreover, he confirms that the demand for more working hands is one of the important reasons for having a higher number of children. Of course, the main objective of demographic research was to examine population growth, but this research has additionally put forward a theoretical explanation for children's contribution to domestic work too. However, this explanation for children's involvement in family work is limited to peasant economies or agrarian societies. The argument developed from this perspective cannot viably be extended to the families in industrialised societies. Given this, the population perspective fails to explain children's work in families at large.

Dominant theoretical explanation for children's work in the family has been put forward from an economic perspective. According to this perspective the economic needs of the family necessitate children's domestic work. With this approach children are considered as economic assets for poor families. The main thrust is on poverty, which is regarded as a compelling factor for children to work in farms and peasant families (Mamdani 1981, Reynolds 1991). The productive and reproductive needs of the peasant family require children for household chores. Adults in these families are directly engaged in productive work and do not find time for domestic chores. Children have to carry out all those domestic chores which adults cannot undertake because of their engagement outside the domestic space. For example, Dube (1988) illustrates that when both parents go out to work on plantations young children have to share the household tasks. She argues that "by performing indispensable household tasks and by minding siblings, a child indirectly contributes to the income-earning activities of the household by freeing the mother or older sibling for work in the field or in the wage sector; or he/she relieves the mother who can then do indispensable domestic work" (1988:201).

Children's domestic work in western countries has been mainly seen from the perspective of socialization. This emphasises the causes and consequences of children's involvement in domestic activities in western countries. The major limitation of this perspective is that it sees children's domestic work only in terms of their development and socialization. It neglects the recognition of its contribution to the division of labour. As psychologists were primarily interested in understanding the individual development of the child, they used the socialization perspective to explain why children are involved in domestic activities; what their motivations are; what is the impact of domestic activities on their own development; and how they are rewarded or punished. For example, Maclelleand (1961) after analyzing children's housework discovered that 'care-taking tasks' served as antecedents of achievement for boys. Relating children's housework to the achievement syndrome, he argued that the reason why children are involved in housework activities is to give them an achievement orientation which will equip them later for the labour market. Similarly, Elder (1974) reasoned that developing responsibility is the purpose of children's household work. Earlier, Winterbottom (1958) had noted that 'expectations on early ages for care-taking clustered with expectations of an early age on items' were related to mastery and to independence in children. Children, therefore, are made to work in order to inculcate freedom of action and skill. Zill and Peterson (1982) also noted the growth in autonomy as an important cause for children's household activities. They found that parents' educational levels gave greater leeway to children's freedom to work. Children were not required to do the 'need tasks' then. In another study Wittner (1980) also finds that children's housework is an index of their socialization as they start learning about the concerns of their parents and other members of the family. Their gradual involvement in household tasks converts them into responsible members of the family. Children's involvement in domestic activities is further seen to develop their cognitive skills (Scribner, 1984; Carraher, 1986) and social qualities (Goodnow 1988). The instance is taken of a potter's son who acquires accelerated skills as he works with his parents (Price-Williams *et. al.,*, 1969). Goodnow and Delaney (1989) find that children's household activities help them even in developing family relationships which is one of the important purposes of the socialization process. Beside the beneficial effects of children's household activities on their development some negative affects have also been noted in this research. Dasen (1980) and Laturey (1980) have found that where parents assign housework which is non-negotiable and, to some extent, compulsory to children, the effect of these tasks is negative on their development.

The early sociological studies have also pursued the socialization perspective for the study of children's housework (Straus 1962; Thrall 1978; Goldstein and Oldham 1979; White and Brinkerhoff 1981; Zelizer 1985). These studies have argued that children's domestic activities are their work-role socialization. The principal focus of these studies was children's activities as an act of learning generational and gender related work roles in the family. Children's housework is examined in terms of the parent-child relationship, where parents are seen as the 'trainer or master' and children the 'trainee or pupil'. (Straus, 1962; Thrall, 1978; White and Brinkerhoff, 1981; and Zelizer, 1985).

Straus (1962) examined the housework of 470 children in Wisconsin (America) on the basis of a cost-benefit ratio. His study finds that the parents assigned regular jobs to children which were undertaken more for their training value than for their productive accomplishment. He finds that children, particularly girls, understand a mother's role in the domestic division of labour through their housework. On the basis of these findings he argues that children's work in the family is more beneficial for themselves than for their parents. Thrall's (1978) study endorses that of Straus. He studied the housework of children of 99 families in Boston (America). The focus of his study was to understand the distribution of stereotypical household tasks in the division of domestic labour. On examining parents' views, Thrall (1978) finds that parents own experiences as children are the basis for the distribution of housework to their own children. Interestingly, his study finds that parents assign household tasks to children to buttress the socialization perspective that children have to do some work primarily for the purpose of training and partly also for developing a sense of belonging to the family. It also suggested that some parents created chores for the children for similar reasons. Thrall says "implicit in this response is the idea that the actual labour contribution of the children is secondary, perhaps even negative" (1978:259). White and Brinkerhoff's (1981) study came as an important landmark in the research of children's domestic work because it noticed children's share in the division of domestic labour. Earlier studies made by Thrall and Straus failed to recognise children's actual labour contribution in the family but this study corrected the imbalance in research on housework which ignored children's role. White and Brinkerhoff's (1981) study was also influenced by the socialization perspective. Like previous studies, this study also examines the parental reports of how housework comes to be allotted in particular ways but goes further to explore what accounts for different patterns of child development. White and Brinkerhoff's (1981) study finds that children start undertaking self-care tasks (such as making their own beds, setting the tables, arranging their toys and the like) at an early age. As they grow older and reach at the age of ten, they move beyond self-centered tasks to family-centered tasks. They shift from helping parents to replacing them by assuming full responsibility (1981:792). They argue that children develop a sense of responsibility and character building through their involvement in housework which is an essential part of their training. The most striking aspect of this research is that it notes, for perhaps the first time, that the meaning of children's housework is not limited to their own development but that their work also has meaning for the family as a whole. Zelizer's (1985) study of American children is worth mentioning in this context. She examines how the 'economically useful' images of the child shift to its 'priceless' recognition. In her examination she finds that children's household activities are neither work nor exploitation but are necessary to raise them as child. Even the case of selling newspapers is called entrepreneurship and extensive work on family farms is exempted as necessary for creating 'unselfishness' and 'family solidarity'. She justifies children's housework on developmental grounds. Her argument is that the usefulness of children's chores is secondary; child work is supposed to train the child, not to help the parents.

Another explanation for children's work in the family has been put forward from an anthropological perspective. This perspective explains children's work in the family with particular reference to the social and cultural practices of communities (Schildkrout 1979, 1980; Nieuwenhuys 1994, 1997). According to this perspective children's work in the family is determined by the social and cultural norms of the family and of the community to which it belongs. The family environment, which is formed by social and cultural ethos, is discussed as an important variable in the determination of children's domestic work. Schildkrout (1980), for example, discusses the work of children of the Hausa-speaking Muslim community of Kano, Nigeria, and describes children's work in terms of particular cultural practices. His study finds that some cultural practices 'necessitate a complement between adult and child roles' (1980:). There is a sea-change in the range of performance of children in such circumstances. The normal performance of children, like running errands for their mothers or working for the maintenance of the household, gets a very wide extension in such cases. The special set of cultural values for women secludes them from society. Evidence in Schildkrout's (1979) study shows that, because of seclusion, the women do not go out of their houses except on rare occasions such as for medical care or social ceremonies. He finds that in such circumstances children have to come forward to take over women's work or to help them. In his study of children's work of the weaving community of Chinnallipatti of South India, George (1990) also finds, like Schildkrout, that there are some instances when children escort women when they go outside the house to hospitals or to visit family friends or relatives. In such circumstances the burden of domestic work on children increases significantly because children become essential links between the women and the outside world.

Nieuwenhuys's (1994) study of children's work in a socio-cultural context also highlights the importance of kinship relationships, familial obligations on cultural grounds and the aura of respectability for children's housework. She studies children from families in a Kerala village of India who were engaged in coir making and fisheries. She argues that 'the standards by which children's work is valued and more generally, the way they are subordinated to seniors, reflect patterns of socialization and, more in general, attitudes with respect to children's role in society' (1994:198). Her study finds that kinship plays a notable role in children's work. She finds that children's activities are not only limited to carrying out the demands of the parents, but they also extend to following the demands of their kin. In fact, these kinship obligations are given primary importance in children's daily routine in and around the house. Thus, culturally legitimized children's subordination in kinship relationship is an important reason for children's involvement in domestic work (Nieuwenhuys 1994). In another study Munroe *et. al.*, (1984) observed the variation in the allocation of work to children and children's subsequent involvement in such work with the degree of kinship. They have studied children of four cultures — *Lagoli* children of Kenya, *Garifuna* children of Belize, *Samoa* children of America and *Newars* children of Nepal — and found that children are less involved in domestic chores where the chores are assigned by the parents, while they are comparatively more involved if chores are assigned by their grandparents. They interpreted the variation in the assignment of chores as a result of closeness and distance in the relationship between child and parents and child and grandparents respectively. This study also finds the difference in children's assigned domestic chores in the families where parents are biological parents and in the families where the parent is surrogate. In the case of biological parents the domestic chores of children are less, while they are more in the case of families of surrogate parents. This suggests that the genealogical distance between children and parents plays a significant role in the determination of children's domestic work. Thus, the anthropological perspective presents a view that the socio-cultural ethos, which determines the child-parent relationships, is the main cause of children's involvement in domestic work. Like others, this perspective also largely ignored the place of children's domestic work in the division of labour.

Factors affecting children's work in the family

The research on children's housework brings out the factors which affect children's involvement. The mother's employment status, ethnic and cultural background, and the child's gender, age and the birth-order are some of the factors which have received the attention of scholars. These will be examined in turn.

Firstly, maternal employment has been seen as a factor which influences the extent and nature of children's involvement in domestic chores. Studies inform us that the mother's employment status is the determining factor for the extent of children's involvement in housework (Proper 1972; Hedges and Barnett 1972; Medrich *et. al.*, 1982; Manke *et. al.*, 1994, Brannen 1995). Hedges and Barnett's study provides evidence that "when a mother takes a job, a portion of her chores are shifted to her children rather than to her husband" (1972:11). Proper's (1972) study finds that the children of working mothers do more housework and for longer hours than the children of non-working mothers. Manke *et. al.*,'s (1994) study finds that children of full-time dual earner families do more housework than the children of part-time dual earner families. Children of single earner families undertake less housework than those of both type of dual earner families. However, Benin and Edward's (1990) study is an exception as it finds that some mothers regard themselves as 'supermoms' and therefore, do not require their children to share the household chores. Hence in this study mothers reported that children's contribution is minimal.

However, this research does not tell us much about the children's experiences of their domestic work. This is so as the majority of studies were based on the information from parents —particularly mothers. Mother's accounts of children's activities in relation to domestic labour represent only a one-sided picture. It is possible that children's accounts of their housework might be the same as their mothers, but we cannot take this for granted. Solberg's (1990) study is certainly noteworthy in this context as it sheds light on this subject. She finds that in such families where parents work outside the home children often leave home last in the morning and return first in the afternoon. Children in such circumstances take possession of the house in their parents' absence. Her study reveals that the absence of parents gave free time to children to undertake as much work as they liked without parental intervention. She noted that children felt more comfortable and did more housework of their own free will in such situations. Morrow's (1996) study also reports that their share of housework increases in the case of maternal employment but she notes that it does not affect their freedom to undertake housework at a desirable time. Looking at this point further research is needed to ascertain children's views in order to understand the link between maternal employment and the constraints and/or opportunities for children for housework.

Secondly, the child's ethnic and cultural background is seen as another significant factor which affects children's housework. In the above discussion we have already noted that few studies find that some cultural practices demand the extra involvement of children in domestic work (Schilderkrout 1980, Brannen 1995). Schildrekrout's (1980) study shows that the *Purdah* (i.e. the seclusion of women), a cultural practice found among the Muslim community of Kano, Nigeria, creates a situation where children have to come forward to help their mothers and other women in carrying out domestic responsibilities. Such cultural practices put an extra burden of housework on children. For example, respect to elders, entertainment of family guests and relatives and kin group obligations are some of the cultural norms of specific ethnic groups of Asians and Middle Eastern countries in Britain which have been found as significant factors for the degree and nature of children's involvement in household chores (Brannen 1995). On the basis of the finding that children of Asian origin are more likely to be involved in domestic chores than their white counterparts, Brannen (1995) argues that the underlying cultural factors are significant to the nature and extent of children's housework. She also notes that culturally determined gender differences among two sets of children are a determining factor in the distribution of domestic work. Her study finds that Asian girls are more involved in non-routine household tasks than the others and Asian boys make their beds more often than the UK born white children. Although Brannen has analysed the notable impact of cultural factors in specific ethnic groups, more efforts are needed to explain how children's experience of domestic work in specific cultural contexts relates to the construction of their childhood.

Thirdly, children's age and birth order have been analysed as important factors in children's domestic work. Age becomes a synonym for ability, both physical and mental, and birth order justifies priorities in the allocation of work. It has been argued that children's age matters in the assignment of domestic chores by parents. Studies find that older children perform more household tasks than younger ones (White and Brinkerhoff 1981; Goldscheider and Waite 1991; Goldstein and Oldham 1979). Goldscheider and Waite find that "as children get older, they clearly become more involved in household chores, in-

and outdoors. Families with teenage children share substantially more housework with their children than families with only preteens. Teenage children are most particularly helpful with yard work, with about equal amounts of sharing from teenage boys and girls" (1991:148). However, when children grow older and reach college age (i.e. 16 and above) their participation in domestic chores decreases (Morrow 1992; Brannen 1995; Berk 1978). So in this way children's age is seen as an important variable for the analysis of children's housework.

Like age, birth order also plays an equally important role in the distribution of housework. Nieuwenhys (1994) finds that the birth order in Poomkara families culturally legitimizes a specific and distinct status for elder and younger children. It is on the basis of this culturally determined status that children's work varies. The seniority and juniority, bound with the respect for and obedience to each other, play a vital role in the distribution of work. They are significant in the type of work given to a particular child too. Brannen (1995) also notes that the birth order of children in the families of Asian origin in Britain plays a significant role in the distribution of housework. She finds, "where there were several children in a household, birth order constituted a frequent excuse given by young people for doing or not doing housework" (1995:330).

While, these studies notice age and birth order as factors which influence children's work, they fail to look at children's capacities to negotiate their position based on age and birth-order within the family. Brannen although noticed the overlapping of age and birth-order in children's housework but she also fails to address the situation in which children negotiate their status on the basis of their substantial and, of course, meaningful contribution to domestic work. This dimension is further investigated in subsequent chapters to know more about children's position in the family.

The last but most significant factor in understanding children's domestic work is gender. A child's gender is found to be one of the fundamental bases for the division of domestic work between boys and girls within the family. Studies both from developing countries and western countries documented this feature in children's domestic work (White and Brinkerhoff 1981; Lynch 1975; Thrall 1978; Berk 1985; Manke *et. al.*, 1994; Solberg 1990; Brannen 1995; Anandlakshami 1990; Bhave 1988; Kanitkar 1996). These studies find that families assign the majority of tasks to children along lines segregated by traditional notions of gender. For example traditionally classified 'feminine chores' such as making bed, cooking, washing dishes, cleaning, laundry and caring go to girls; while 'masculine chores' such as repairing, grocery shopping, mowing the grass, washing the car go to boys. For example Goldstein and Oldham's (1979) study found that girls are more likely to help with kitchen work and wash and dry dishes, while boys are more likely to remove trash and do errands. These studies also find that girls do more jobs than boys. For example Brannen (1995) found that girls perform eleven out of the thirteen listed household tasks more frequently than boys. Not only this, but the amount of work and the time spent on it is also significantly different between girls and boys (Goldscheider and Waite1991). According to mothers of children, Berk (1985) reports, girls do twice as many household tasks as boys. White and Brinkerhoff's (1981) study provides evidence that girls spend two hours more per week on housework than boys. The research also shows that the quantitative and qualitative difference between genders begins at a very early age.

More importantly, these studies show that children accommodate the gender construction in their childhood through the division of domestic work on gender lines. In her study of 200 school girls of 13 to 15 years in Pune (India) Kanitkar (1996) finds that "girls have been conditioned to think traditionally in that all chores within the house as fetching water were considered as a woman's prerogative" (1996:36). The research to date reveals that gender plays a decisive role in the assignment of domestic chores and that children undertake gender segregated work roles. However, this research does not explain how gender is constructed through domestic work or how children use their gendered identity in negotiating their domestic work. To answer these equally important questions children's experience of domestic work on gender lines should be ascertained. The meanings they draw and attach to their domestic work with special reference to gender are explored in the subsequent chapters.

Use and abuse of children's work in the family

It is commonly believed that children's housework is either positively beneficial for children's development or at least non-exploitative. This is assumed because the work is normally performed under the supervision of parents who are considered as guardians of the best interest of the child. With this assumption, scholars have not suspected any kind of exploitation of children in the context of housework. However, the few studies which go into the details of children's family life find that this is not the case. Children's accounts tell a different story. For example, Nieuwenhuys (1995) finds that children's subordination to kinship obligations does not easily permit their work to be appreciated in its own right. Their subservience becomes coercion too. Because of the hierarchy of status within the family children's work is accorded a lower value. Children are always on the bottom rung of the hierarchical ladder while parents are at the top. Sometimes this low status decides the quality of the child's work in the family too. This suggests that children's domestic work is sometimes as exploitative as the work in waged employment because the worker does not get the due meanings because of their subordinate position. However, the desirability of that work is the same as that of others' work in the family.

The research on children's domestic work is also largely silent on the issue of the use of it by children. Except Solberg (1990), who notes that children negotiate their status and position in performing their household responsibilities, no study acknowledged that children are consciously involved in domestic work and that they make use of it for their own purposes. Few psychological studies have mentioned that children work in the family because they want to help their parents (Eisenberg *et. al.*, 1985; Grusec 1982, 1985). From children's accounts Eisenberg *et. al.*, (1985) have pointed out that children work to help or assist others and that this is based on obedience and the concepts of reward and punishment. Grusec (1982) argues that children's 'offer' to work is a sign of their pro-social behaviour. According to him the three forms of social behaviour—helping, sharing and showing concern are the principal reasons for children's involvement in household chores (Coded in Goodnow, 1988). Children's ability to work (Goodnow 1984), their offer to help and their concern for family affairs (Grusec 1982; Eisenberg *et. al.*, 1985) are positive signs of their emergent agency. Children's savoir-faire is a promising sign of their potential character as contributors in their own right. However, the over-commitment to the outcome of the socialization process, which looms large in the literature, fails to recognize as something intrinsically significant for children themselves.

Sociology of childhood and children's domestic work

The socialization perspective on children's work in the family has been criticised in the last decade, mainly on two grounds. Firstly, the approach of taking children as 'recipients' in the socialization process was found to be incomplete. This approach does not allow us to see children as active participants in their own right. However, some studies have found that children do 'help' or 'assist' their parents in household chores. But their help or assistance is seen as an important step in developing a sense of responsibility and character building. More recent studies have shown that children not only help their parents but they replace their parents in domestic work (Morrow 1992; Solberg 1990). This suggests that to see children's domestic work as only work role-rehearsal is incorrect. Children's role as active agents needs to be built into analysis of children's involvement in domestic work.

Those who look at children as actors find that they

contribute to the domestic work order in a socially meaningful way. For example, Solberg's study, based on the data collected in Norway during a period of ten years, provided strong empirical evidence of children's work, particularly in relation to household management. Her findings show that domestic work is shared not only between parents, but also by children (Solberg and Vestby, 1987; Solberg, 1987). She points out that mothers' workload in domestic tasks in Norway has diminished in the last decades because of their increased participation in the labour force but that fathers' share in it has not increased. Her argument is that children's share in domestic work has substantially increased during these years and that the mother's workload has been transferred to the children. In this way, she finds that children's share in domestic work comes closer to their mothers' (Solberg, 1990). Her study also finds that children's negotiating capacity has increased in the household management which, she argues, helps them to define and construct their own childhood by means of their participation in domestic work (Solberg, 1990). Morrow's (1992) study in Britain merits significant attention in this context, as it challenges the conventional approach to children and their work. She rejects the notion of children's overall dependence in the family and provides evidence to prove the 'interdependence' between children and parents in relation to domestic work. Out of four categories of children's work noticed by Morrow (1994) only two - the 'non-domestic family labour' and the 'domestic labour' —are relevant in the present context. She has found 'about 30 per cent of the boys in the sample and 50 per cent of the girls described undertaking some form of domestic labour' while "10 per cent of the children who worked described doing so for their family businesses" (1994:132). Morrow argues that children are not only caring for siblings but they also care for parents and grandparents, so contradicting the common notion that children's existence in the household increases the workload of parents. It shows that instead of being 'burdens' on the family they also contribute to it. Theoretically, Solberg's and Morrow's study are pointers to a shift in perspective on children's domestic work. This shift is important as it moves the direction of the study of children's work in the family from 'recipient' child to 'contributor' child.

The second and most forceful criticism of the socialization perspective on children's domestic work was the lack of children's perspective on their work. We have already noticed that the main informants on children's housework are adults (mainly parents). It is noticeable that children have not been used even as sounding boards for the information gathered through adults. If at all they have been tapped during data collection the exercise has been characterised by asking them to report only the number of tasks they perform, their opinion has not been allowed to interfere in the process. Morrow's (1994) and Solberg's (1990) study highlights the latent promise for future analysis of letting the children speaks on the issue of their domestic work. In this way, the sociology of childhood emerged as a criticism of the socialization perspective, considers children as potential contributors to the domestic work order. However, this perspective is currently limited by the absence of any detailed study on children's domestic work, from the viewpoint of children themselves.

The above discussion identifies a number of issues of use in developing a framework for exploring children's domestic work. In the light of above discussion it can be ascertained that children's work in the family is not a subject to be subsumed under the socialization process. The existing evidence points out that children's contribution to domestic work from 'assistance' and 'help' to 'substitution' are all important milestones in the actual realization of the value of their work. Its significance in the context of personal development is only a small acceptance of what it means when judged against the social context i.e. how it adds to the value of work by others and the family as a whole. The importance of children's work is described by Nieuwenhuys as being like a 'small wheel' in the domestic economy (1994: 198). However, the predominant strain in most of the psychological and sociological literature, particularly in western countries, is that the child's activities at home are part of his/her socialization; as an instrument of developing responsibility and morality (Goodnow 1988, 1989); as an achievement orientation for future labour force (McClelland 1961); as a role-rehearsal of future adult (Goldstein and Oldham 1979). This has been a limitation in acknowledging or evaluating the actual contribution of children to domestic work. However, the latest research provides sporadic glimpses of children's actorship. Children's help or assistance to parents in domestic chores is seen as a step further. Researchers observed that their work is 'exchangeable' with adults. The argument is that children do housework as 'responsible' members (Seymour 1988, George 1990, Morrow, 1994) and offer their services to elders, sometimes even as 'substitutes' for indispensable family tasks (Solberg, 1990, Morrow, 1992). These findings pose fundamental questions: does work belong to children's family life? is this work socially meaningful? if yes then what is the position of children in the division of labour? To answer these questions it is now necessary to investigate various issues related to children's domestic work and to analyse them from the children's perspectives. This is the primary objective of the empirical study to which we now turn.

3

CHILDREN'S DOMESTIC WORK
Towards A Theoretical Conceptualisation

Until the beginning of 1990s children were figured in sociological studies to understand the institutions around them, mainly the family and the school. The focus of these studies was to examine how these institutions influence the child's socialization. Children were only the subject of observations not as the subjects in their own right. This results in the marginalisation of children in sociological discourse. This happened, as Alanen (1988) explains, because of the closely knitted triangular concepts of childhood, the family and socialization. These theree concepts were interwoven in such a way that it was not possible to see children as independent subjects. Children were 'kept in a waiting position' for the analysis as independent subjects "until they can be classified as 'adults', living and competing in adult society" (Qvortrup 1985:132). In the last decade a new debate has emerged to see children as subjects in their own right. This debate looked at children as structural entities and examined their work in relation to society and to their childhood.

To examine the marginalisation of children in early sociological studies it is necessary to take into account the prominent approaches from the start to understand the present thoerisation of children and their work. With the objective to grasp the understanding of children's theoretical position we discuss it from the early theorization and note the drift of change marked in perspective. The available perspectives of study for the child have all relevance in the mediate and immediate background. For a comprehensive understanding of the available approaches, their outstanding features as well as their limitations are examined. The principal task we have set in this chapter is to develop a theoretical conception of children's domestic work. Our discussion takes up latest developments in the sociology of childhood which assumes that children have agency. Discussing children as actors and theorising their work in the family is a central issue of this endeavour. Whether the popular notion of work can apply to children and family are examined and the role of children's work is discussed in the construction of childhood, society and its economy. In this process the potential of children's agency in creating childhood as well as contributing social structure becomes apparent. During this discourse the concepts of responsibility and autonomy are developed as conceptual tools for the exploration of meaning and significance of children's domestic work. Our primary concern here is to trace how a child's domestic work contributes to the achievement of autonomous agency rather than how autonomy affects child's work.

SECTION I

The Study of the Child: The Theoretical Stages

The concern for the study of the child can be distinguished into two distinctive theoretical stages. The first theoretical stage, which dominated for fairly long period, explains the child through socialisation theory. Within this theoretical approach children were regarded as incompetent, immature and irrational humans which need to be socialised. The process through which they have been converted as competent, mature and rational social actors is explained as socialisation process. The second and the latest theoretical approach, that emerged through the criticism of socialisation theory, considers children as actors in their own right. This approach explains that because of the social construction of children's incompetence and dependence they have not been recognised as a social category. The major argument of this theoretical explanation is that children are active members of society and have a distinct social position. Both theoretical stages are discussed below in greater detail.

Theory of Socialisation

The evolution of theory of socialisation can be traced in the images of the child propounded by sixteenth and seventeenth century western philosophers. The dominant ideology during this period has separated 'the child' from the mainstream society with which he/she had to be integrated. St. Augustine's notion of the *'original sin'*, for example, referred to children as 'weak and innately prone to sin and corruption' (see for detail Gittins 1998:146-152). This philosophical statement set the stage for strict discipline and control over children by adults in society. In the late seventeenth century John Locke's concern with children shifted the direction of discourse. Locke denied inborn knowledge and argued that human experiences driven from all possible forms of knowledge. On children, Locke's argument was that they are *tabula rasa*. His belief was that children are empty buckets or blank sheets which were filled by experiences. He maintained that all children are imperfect and incomplete version of adults and childhood is a stage whose end is adulthood. In the eighteenth century, Rousseau also argued that children are born innocent and need adult supervision and guidance. They are corrupted by society. Children were either regarded as innocent and malleable or as sinful who had to be corrected. This view led to the idea that children are biologically given and thus 'natural'.

The problem (that children need correct training and guidance) arising out of this theoretical position of children demanded a solution. It was in response to this concern that education appeared to provide an obvious solution for the 'needy' as well as the 'wild' children. The period of eighteenth and nineteenth century saw a mushrooming of educational institutions in the west. The debate began on how to tailor education to meet the needs of the children and society. Both the family (the site of children's first interactions with their social world) and the school (where children are first introduced to the formal world) gained importance in the discussions. The ideational currents that produced in these institutions had separated the children from the society and placed them either in the family and or in the school. These currents dominated until the second half of the twentieth century. The circumstances and the process through which children were supposed to be re-inducted into society and made congruent to it provided the landscape for the theory of socialisation. The measures instrumental to the transformation of the child in order to fit in the society all formed the ingredients of socialisation theory. Thus, "both the term and the concept of socialisation originally emerged as a corollary of the concept of society, in an age when arguments for a separate scientific discipline of sociology were being advanced" (Alanen 1988:57).

Historically, the term 'socialization' came to be used for the study of the child in sociology and psychology at almost the same time. However, the emphasis was different in both the disciplines. In sociology, the socialisation process has been studied with reference to society and culture while in psychology the emphasis was on the child's individual development. Despite the difference in their focus, both the disciplines have consensus on one point that children are 'not adult' and therefore, are dependent on adults. Clausen (1968) noted that socialisation theory formally emerged as a theoretical tool, during 1930 to 1950 in the discourse of American positivism, to understand the process by which children internalise social values. This was given further impetus by

Talcott Parsons, the chief spokesman of the functionalist theory during the 1950s and 1960s, through a focua on the two features involved in a child's 'needs disposition': the performance of an act and satisfaction. He observed the greater good for the society through the interplay of a child's desire and constraints. An important concept developed in his socialisation theory is 'identification' (Parsons 1951). The social norms, according to him, are a source of 'identity' between the individual actor and the social system. This identification accounts for their recognition as members of the social system, their commitments to the social order and also for their behavioural coherence. Parsons consider the family as a key for socialisation. Thus, socialisation signifies two characteristic features in the Parsonian model: firstly, the transmission of culture and secondly, the process of being human through interaction with others. Children were seen, in this functionalist endeavour, as an important pre-requisite for the maintenance and continuance of functioning of society (Inkeles 1968).

The Major Limitations of Socialisation Theory

Socialisation theory remained in currency for a fairly long period. Until the first half of the 1980s the hegemony of socialization theory was dominated all the major branches of social sciences dealing with the study of children. Only a few attempts have been made to challenge this dominance (e.g. Dreitzel 1973; Denzin 1977; Jenks 1982). However, the period of late 1980s a growing body of critical comments appeared (e.g., Ambert 1986;Qvortrup 1985; Alanen 1988; Stainton-Rogers *et. al.*, 1989) that focused on the two main grounds: firstly, the over-emphasis on child's development through various stages which led inevitably to the ignorance of children's capacities as actors and secondly, the dominance of an adult's perspective and a failure to recognise the legitimacy of children's views and experiences related to their social life.

Socialization theory chiefly emphasises children's development. The role of family and school, and other social institutions in children's socialization and development have been discussed. For instance, in the family attention was paid for the training of the child to equip him/her with the social norms and values that enable him/her to become an acceptable member of the society in future. Similarly, in schools attention was paid to the education required to transform the child into a good adult worker. In this approach children were studied primarily in terms of their result or end state. Social institutions become important because they decide what children are expected 'to become' and to transform children into the desired form of adults. Here children's present state of 'being' is considered to be an empty bucket which is to be filled by a 'cultural dope' through training. Thus the socialization theory positioned children as passive objects and regarded their childhood "as a stage of life that builds preparatory mechanism into the child's behaviour so that he is gradually equipped with the competence to participate in everyday activities" (Speir 1982:181). This assumption regarded children's sharp corners as in need of pruning to make them fit into civilised society. The child, in this way, has been considered as the precursor of the civilised adult.

This neglect of the present state of the child in socialization theory has been criticised. It has been argued that "in sociology the concept of socialization acts as a kind of suppresser of childhood's present tense, orientating analysis either towards the past (what went wrong with socialisation) or the future (what the goals of socialisation should be)" (James *et. al.*, 1998:28). The socialisation theory basically monopolised the concept of development and relegated the child to an abject passive state. The unquestionable mandates of all powerful adults, issued in unidimensional social relationships for children who were taught always to truckle to adults, created an atmosphere of silent submission. This was sufficient to stifle any attempt to react. Commenting on adult's manipulation of children, Jenks says that "this unilateral manipulation of children within socialization theories condemns them to the permanent conceptual status of absent presence. Ironically in relation to their actual intrusions into the best-laid plans of aspiration, children are depotentiated within socialisation theory, they become nominal ciphers seemingly without an active dimension" (1996:10).

The way of looking at the child as passive object ignores his or her capacity to act on their own. The passiveness of the child does not require him or her to react in any way and that is why he or she is expected to internalise all the matter which is placed before him or her by adults. The child's reactive and interactive capacities in social situations are glossed over and their meaningful interactions are overlooked. The child's active participation in social processes is precluded either purposefully or on the presumption that his/her interests do not coalesce with those of adults. The avowed concern for the process under the socialization theory is neglected in actuality because it overlooks the possibility of children's own contribution as active participants. It is confined to internalisation — an idea which remains deficient in view of the limitations during the process — which is not a one way process (Corsaro 1997). Thus, it offers an over simplistic view.

The second major ground of criticism of socialisation theory is its adultist perspective. The socialization theory predominantly looked at adults' interests in children. Adults' have their own interests and they tailor social institutions to reproduce themselves. They, therefore, influence children in order to secure their interests conducive to their aim of reproduction. For instance, in a family parents are the persons who try to reproduce their interests in children while in school, teachers try to do the same. In total, socialization theory explains the child from an adults' point of view.

The New Sociology of Childhood

Through criticism of the socialisation theory an alternative sociological approach has emerged to provide a fertile ground for the study of the children as independent subjects. During the 1980s and 1990s the mainstream sociological theory was dominated by the structuralist and post-structuralist debates that argue that society is to be understood in terms of 'structures' and 'agency' respectively. James and Prout (1990), in their work on social construction and re-construction of childhood, made a strong case for the post-structuralist position. They argue that the children should be studied as a social and cultural category just like any other. Qvortrup and others' (1994) in the structuralist approach have also argued that children constitute a permanent structure of every society. Children's views should be interpreted not only in their own context but also in relation to other social structures, 'as a kind of intertextuality' (Editorial 1999: Childhood).

The emergence of this new idea in the context of children, and concerned with childhood as belonging to children, marks a departure from the previous predominant genre of literature. James and others (1998) have aptly described this as a process of transitional theorising that stretches from the concepts of *'pre-sociological child'* to *'sociological child'*. This new sociological approach sees children as active social actors grounded on six basic tenets, as first proposed by James and Prout (1990) and later endorsed by Jenks (1996) and Mayall (1996) in their work. They are as follows:

- The child and childhood is a social construction rather than a biological and natural category. Children form a distinctive social group with specific structural and cultural expressions.
- Childhood varies according to specific culture and therefore exists in a plurality of forms. The emphasis is therefore, on various childhoods and not one universal childhood. Childhood is as good a variable of social analysis as any other like class, gender, etc.
- It is not only the interest of adults that in the construction of childhood. Children are real entity and have their own interests. There is always interplay between the interest of children and others and the social relations that they involve. Since children are found to have both social relationship and their own

sub-cultures, they are worthy of independent study in their own right.

- Children are social actors who construct their own lives, the lives of those around them and their societies as well.
- Children are not mere beneficiaries of economic resources but are contributors to societal resources and engaged in production.
- Children are both actors and participants and therefore have a right to a 'voice'. The meaning that social life has should filter down to its participants as well as for which the ethnographic methodology is found useful.

In sum, the basic assumption of the new sociological theory is that childhood is exposed to the same societal forces as adulthood. It assumes that like adults, children participate in society's organised activities either in the form of economic production or consumption. It also assumes that both children and adults affect each other, as well as those events occurring in wider society. They are also influenced by developments taking place in society like greater participation in the labour force by women or dissolution of traditional families.

SECTION II
Children and Work

Socialisation theory, as noted in the above section, considers the child as a meek, mute and malleable person in need of nurturing and care. Their activities are explained in terms of their development. The question whether it was at all possible for children to work or that it was implied in children's agency to work under specific structures, were never considered within the socialisation approach. However, the new sociological approach discussed above has created the possibility for analysis of "children's work within the political economy of particular localities and their connections into regional and global systems of production, exchange and distribution"

(James *et. al.,* 1998: 102-3). The understanding of children's work which is formed by its mutual interchange with socio-economic forces allows for consideration of children as actively embedded in the division of labour (Qvortrup 1994a). Children's activities have been located in societal economy. For example, children's school activities in the western countries are in form of socio-economic activity in some ways equivalent, to classical child labour. This argument not only emphasises children as actors, it also argues that children's activities are systematically exploited by adults too. For example, Oldman (1994) points out that child's activities produce adult's 'childwork'. He maintains that adults' interests, that are different from children's interests, are to occupy children with a number of different activities in order to create paid jobs for adults. So, children's activities in school or in 'children's job' are considered economically significant for adults. In contrast to the structural approach that regards children and adults as separate groups having their specific interests, this approach advocates the idea of looking at children's work in relation to their structural existence in the wider division of labour in society.

Children's Work and Society

The role of children's work in society's division of labour has been ignored in the social construction of the modern childhood. It has been noted that children's participation in the waged labour market largely ended during the nineteenth and early twentieth century on the grounds of their socially constructed incompetence and their direct productive roles were withdrawn (Qvortrup 1994). As the socialisation approach emphasises children's development it neglects the importance of children's work for society's organisation. The social construction of childhood was directed towards the separation of children from adult society. In this process children's immediate contribution to society was devalued, while they were seen as assets of future. Zelizer (1985) maintained that children's previous usefulness is converted to a present uselessness, thus positioning children as 'priceless'. This conceptualisation, however, has been challenged in the sociology of childhood. Scholars posed a question on the absence of children from the division of labour. For example, Qvortrup (1985) argues that children's placement in the school does not mean their exclusion from the division of labour since school labour is also a form of work. According to him only the form of children's labour has changed from classical child labour to school work. "Children's school activities, as they are organised systematically by adults and continuously adapted to new modern conditions of technology and economy, must in principle be understood as the continuation of child labour of previous modes of production' (Qvortrup 1994:334). It has been argued that children's school labour is an integral part of societal division of labour, thus, children contribute to 'human capital formation" (1994:23). This argument rejects the idea that children are moved from useless to useful status as argued by Zelizer (1985), and maintains that children are a permanent and significant component of the society.

Children's activities are of paramount importance for adults. Whether it is in the developed world or developing we can see that children are an important segment of the social life. If children are dependants on adults in society, as argued by socialisation theory, adults also depend on children in other ways. Oldman (1994) pointed out how adults and other social structures depend upon children for their interests by arguing that 'childwork' (the work done by adults for children) of adults is an important economic activity in the industrial world. Child-care has been developed as an economically gainful activity both within and outside the family. Initially it is adults who create jobs engaged with children (e.g. schools, nurseries, institutional caring etc.) and use them for their economic gains. This is not to say that children's interest is not fulfilled in these institution but these institutions serve the interests of both. Furthermore, Oldman (1994) maintains that adults and children constitute different classes on the basis of their different sets of interests. The point here is not so much whether we agree or not with Oldman's argumer.: but that it cannot be denied that children's activities have social and economic value for adults. Thus children's activities affect and are affected by social and economic interests of other structures of society.

The social and economic value of children's activities can be ascertained in the family circumstances too. Children are seen either directly helping in the family business for example in Chinese take away businesses in Britain, where they work as interpreters or helpers to their Chinese speaking parents (Song, 1995). They are also indirectly involved in taking over their parents household responsibilities to free them to undertake economic activities especially in case of maternal employment (Morrow, 1992). Thus, children's activities in the families might not produce the direct economic return, as in the market economy, but these activities do influence the balance between adults' participation in the labour market and their contribution to domestic labour.

Children's work is found significant in producing and reproducing social relationships too. The role of children's work in the social dynamics of Hausa people of Kano in Nigeria is exemplified by Schildkrout (1975). She found that children were playing an important role in maintaining the *Purdah* system in which women were excluded from communicating with mainstream social life. With this tradition women are not permitted to attend the visitors in the family; they can move only with female relatives or friends; and they are not allowed to attend the social gatherings such as birth ceremonies, marriages, or funerals. Men also have to keep a social distance from women. It is in this context that "Hausa children enjoy a freedom that no other group in the society commands—the right to wander in and out of people's houses. Children are not expected to observe formal greetings behaviour, and they casually walk into the houses of neighbour, relatives, friends and even strangers, to look for playmates, to make purchases, to offer things for sale, or to carry message" (1975:124). Hausa children demonstrate how through their work they contribute solidly to the maintenance of the social order of the family and community.

The contribution of children to the maintenance of social order can also be perceived in the societies of developing countries where it is common for children to take a substantial part in work essential for the subsistence of the family. The child labour debate also at least agrees that children's work in most situations is an economic necessity in developing countries. Children's involvement in various paid and unpaid work activities maintains and fulfils the social and economic needs of the family. This also suggests that child labour, if not in hazardous industrial conditions, helps the maintenance of social order of local communities as well.

Nieuwenhuys's (1994) work on Poomkara children of Kerala, India is another example of children's work for the construction of society. In her two years of extensive fieldwork she found that these children start work from a very early age and gradually take over the work responsibilities of adults. Their work is not merely essential for the family economy but 'this has sustained their resilience in the face of technical modernisation' (1994:201). Except for the crucial help in maintaining and extending families income, the very existence of family stand in danger of extinction because of technological advances. Another important finding of her research is that work undertaken by children created confidence in them and led to social mobility. They covered long distances away from home to work in the coir and fishing industry. This practice not only meant more work and money but it augmented the social status of the family in the eyes of local community. An important feature of Poomkara children's work noted by Nieuwenhuys is that kinship obligations help in the household activities. This helps them "in achieving social status of the kin's because of the role of the children" (1994:199).

What is material in the example is the way it illustrates firstly, the degree of the agency of among children and secondly, their contribution not only to the maintenance of the social order, but also to its resilience and reproduction. Lastly, the children are also involved in an extensive area of activity that goes beyond the immediate family structure and makes a positive contribution to the family structure of other component of the society that is kin whose social status is upgraded because of their work. Such multiple consequences of children's work in the maintenance and upgrading of social structures is difficult else where.

Children's Work and their Childhood

For fairly long period, the principal question asked about children's work has been its impact on their health and development. Until the 1990's the child labour debate was usually devoted towards this query. Some researchers started exploring how children's work is meaningful for their own childhood (see Boyden *et. al.*, 1998). It is found that they carry out various types of work both in a personal and social context in their own capacities and abilities. It is their work which provides a chance for them to realise the social presence and subsequently shape their childhood. For instance, children are seen working in the family either singly or along with others. When they participate in a joint family experience by being actively involved with others in carrying out household tasks it becomes easier to see how they contribute to the creation of their own childhood. For example, the responsibility of care of younger children is shared by older siblings and parents in India (Dube 1988). This practice provides an opportunity for children to participate in the daily family life as responsible members. Of course, their childhood is different from those children where they are not involved in such activities. Therefore, children shape their childhood by participating or not participating in various tasks.

The forms of involvement in various tasks through which children realise their agency and give shape to their childhood differs in various social classes. Children born in the poor families are often brought up under circumstances which demand hard work from a very young age. Their childhood is naturally different from those who are born in affluent class. Similarly, childhood in rural and urban areas also differ because of the life-chances. Children in rural areas have more opportunities to work and share with their parents. This is a strange situation as children's work in the farm has not been effectively addressed in social legislation and they still work in farms and houses even in western countries too. However, the legislation prohibits children's work in paid employment in urban areas and as paid employment is mainly located in urban areas, these children are effectively prevented from working with adults. This pattern suggests that childhood in urban areas are definitely different from rural areas because of the opportunities and circumstances of involvement of children in work. In this way it is clear that the different social situations provide different opportunities to children for realising their agency, which consequently shapes their childhood.

In the construction of their childhood children also use and negotiate their social position, power and status through their work in different situations. Children as a social structure negotiate their position through their work with other social structures so as to construct their childhood. For example, a child negotiates its position and power in the family with other adult members as well as with peers through his/her contribution to domestic work. Julia Brannen (1995) examined parents and young people to find out how they negotiate their contribution to and their exemption from housework which gives an empirical basis in support of the above argument.

We have noted earlier that research on children's work at home has shown that where only one parent is working in dual parent families children's contribution to work is less than in families where both parents are working. The dependency of children on adults in both the cases is also different. It is thus the agency of the child and its expression which makes for the vital change in the form of its childhood and which at the same time strengthens or weakens child's relationships with an adult. Morrow (1992) has shown that in the inter-dependency of child and parents in terms of housework children command a different position of power and have a wider scope to display their agency. Thus, through their work children play a significant role in the construction of their childhood.

Children and Domestic Work

In conventional economics the market and households have been separated. Under this dualism, work has been defined as a paid activity linked to the market economy whereas household work has been marginalised. This marginalisation poses serious problems when the unpaid household activities started replacing paid work during the growth of specialisations in economies of the West. Feminist scholars (both Marxist feminist and socialist feminist) have questioned the separation of households and markets and its exclusion of domestic work from analysis (see Gardiner 1995). Marxist feminist have emphasised importance of unpaid domestic work for the reproduction of the labour force and socialist feminist analysis was mainly focused on gender and power relations. Despite the difference on emphasis, these scholars have provided important insights into the status of domestic work. Most importantly they have documented the economic value of domestic work and rendered it socially and economically significant. Within this debate, domestic labour was identified as socially necessary yet unpaid/ unrewarded labour carried out by women and primarily for the benefit of capital and men.

The problem of this history of neglect stems from the way 'work' has been defined. A reading of the history of work shows that work has numerous meanings. Therefore defining work is not easy and even the distinction between 'work' and 'non-work', which prima facie may appear simple, is not always so. The connotations that the word 'work' acquires directly affect the meanings of 'non-work' too. Household repair and maintenance activities, for instance, by a family member has not been called work although it is paid as work when done by an outsider. It is intriguing to find that the task of caring when performed by an outsider is called 'paid work'; when performed by mother it is described as 'unpaid work', but when it is carried out by an elder child it is relegated to the category of 'no-work' or 'assistance'. This subtle shift in the interpretation is attributable to the change in the context and the perspective adopted. Grint (1998) has also pointed out that work may appear opposed to 'leisure' but it would be difficult to regard 'non-work' always as 'leisure'. Schwimmer (1979) explains this difficulty in the distinction between 'work' and 'non-work' for the case of an artist. The same activity is looked upon as 'non-work' in one perspective; 'work' in another perspective; and 'leisure' in yet another perspective. Noting the difficulty Grint (1998) maintains that every household activity which is done gratis can also be done for money in formal economy. As such a distinction between 'work' and "non-work' is dubious. Starting with Joyce's caution that the 'conventional model of work as paid employment should not be taken as normal" Grint (1998) argues that "in essence, work is a socially constructed phenomenon without fixed or universal meaning across space and time but its meanings are delimited by the cultural forms in which it is practiced". Grint's definition of work thus suggests that the notion of work cannot be universalized because, firstly, it is a socially constructed phenomenon and therefore changes from society to society; and secondly, the cultural context in which work takes place is also bound to be different. The implication is that there cannot be an objective assessment of work and the meaning cannot be assumed to be self-evident. Its intrinsic nature can be discerned only through studies that are sensitive to specific cultural conditions.

Ransom (1996) however, does not attempt to outline the broad criteria that characterize work. These criteria are mental/ physical exertion; purposeful expedient activity; activity that is economically valuable; and a public activity. Since individual's very existence depends upon action the criterion of mental and physical exertion covers the basic motivation of work. It is also a common knowledge that a person does not live by bread alone but has an aim in life to fulfill and a desire to express his/her creativity. This elemental motivation results in the choice of criterion as a purposeful expedient activity. Performance in return for wages is a quality which responds directly to the basic needs of security of life. Individual not only work for themselves but their output is set for exchange in the market. Many do valuable work at home. Therefore, it is not the substance or nature of an activity but its exchangeability that matters. In this way the needs of others and the exchangeability of work justifies the expectation of social contact reflected in the criterion of public activity. The range of needs includes not only the basic ones but also higher needs of creativity which call for social relations and interaction and also justify a different scale of usefulness and value.

Goodnow's (1988) delineation of the features of children's work is in tune with Ransom's criteria of work. According to him, children's activity should be counted as 'work' if it required efforts, is deemed useful by others and involves interactions with others, either in helping them to achieve their goals or seeking to help others. James and Prout (1997), following Wadel (1979) and Wallman (1979) also recommend a more expansive definition of work including activities "which involve the production, management and conversion of resources—whether these be materials, ideas or people" (1997: 241).

To sum the above discussion, work need to be understood as an activity motivated by our needs in accordance with our capacity and express through action involving production, management and conversion of resources of materials, ideas or people. This enlarged definition covers all aspects of activities which could be understood as work. This definition of work is an important lens through which to view children's involvement in family work. If they live not only for the future, but also for the present, their domestic work has a present relevance. Children's activities in the family are not only described in a developmental context, but also as closely linked with the work of others in the family. It is through work that children not only affect others but are also affected by it themselves. It has a value to be gathered through social relationships.

Now the question is to what extent children's activities in the family resemble the criterion discussed above. To be categorized as work children's domestic activities must appear to be an integral part of the social and economic order of the family in terms of production, management and conversion of resources. There are studies in which children's domestic activities including sibling care form an essential part of the domestic work order (e.g., Solberg 1990; Mayall, 1996). Generally it is assumed to be mother's work but it is frequently done by children. This involvement of children in the family activity is directly beneficial to the family-system. From this, at least, one indisputable inference would be that activities such as caring should be regarded as 'work' because they are socially necessary forms of labour.

An activity is work when it not only influences the system where it takes place but it also influences the doer, in some way or other. The doer is influenced in terms of some return of their activity. With this characteristic feature of work, when we examine children's domestic activities, it is important to see whether children get any return of their organised activities in the domestic space. The socialisation theory already determines that children's household activities, in return, help them in developing as adults. This return need not necessarily be purely economic (as in the case of women's domestic labour). On the other hand, the interpretative approach finds that children's participation in household work not only develops them into responsible members, but also increases their agency as is recognised as such by the fact of negotiating capacities of the children (Solberg, 1990).

Another reason to qualify children's domestic activities as work is an examination of whether they influence the social structure through their household activities. Before this we have to see whether children's domestic activities have any productive or reproductive value. Children, especially girls, take part in family chores by actively assisting mothers both in the kitchen as well as nurturing siblings. Their contribution represents a direct involvement in socially productive work. There is some evidence that children have to carry out the household activities independently too. However, this experience stands them in good stead as parents (particularly mothers) who reproduce these activities independently. This suggests the reproductive value of their work like in the case of women. How children's productive and reproductive work influences the social structure has been exemplified in the earlier reference to Schildkrout's (1980) study of Hausa children. Clearly, children's domestic activities share the qualities of 'work' such as organised, beneficial to the system, giving a return to the doer and influencing the social structure.

The question that therefore arises is how children involve themselves in the domestic work. Is it a conscious involvement and if so, how does it contribute to the social order of the family? Generally speaking children's domestic activities can be classified into those activities taken up in compliance of family dictates and those carried out under their own free will. Those falling under the first classification also imply a cognitive base which again presumes conscious application of mind. Under the socialisation paradigm it may be noted that children who do not develop as desired are seen as deviants. It does not signify lack of cognition or consciousness but aberrant or erratic behaviour. As regards work done under their own free will, their conscious application is also implied. Mayall's (1996) study is the strongest example of this in which she finds that the children, even from the age of two contribute to the maintenance of social order of the family through various activities including self-care. She finds that children's activities maintain the home and construct and reconstruct family relations. This suggests that if young children have been found to contribute to the maintenance and the reproduction of the family, older children would almost certainly have a greater involvement. Solberg's (1987) study of children's work in Norwegian families also shows that children's contribution to domestic work can complement the contributions of their mothers. These findings support the present suggestion that children's domestic work is a conscious contribution to the organization of the family.

Another aspect of children's domestic work is how far we rely on the information of provided by children themselves. Studies on children's activities in the family under the socialisation paradigm predominantly rely on data gathered from adults, mainly parents. Children's activities have been assessed on the evidence of others but not from the point of view of children. How much children contribute to domestic work as an active social agent is uncertain because children's view on desirability and utility of their contributions have received little attention. The most vital issue — children's own experiences of domestic work — has been missing throughout the research. However, some studies in the recent past do demonstrate that children are productive in the home. At this juncture the question of whether children contribute to domestic work out of free will or necessity becomes important. When we deal with this question the prevailing notions of family obligations and discipline give one set of answers, while the notion of individual responsibility provides another set. For example, Solberg's (1990) study finds that children do much work in the absence of their parents, which she suggests is so because children feel more responsible and autonomous in this situation. Whether or not this is a consequence of children's autonomy or compliance with strict family discipline is another question. These two situations—*responsibility and obligation; autonomy and independence*—must be theoretically resolved in order to comprehend children's relationship to domestic work. For this reason, children's experiences become primordial and its empirical examination turns out to be of great importance to any understanding of children's life.

The Conceptual Tools for the Explanation of Children's Domestic Work

For the study of children's domestic work, a number of tools are required to clarify the conceptual status of children's domestic activities. These are, firstly, responsibility and obligation. The notions of responsibility and obligations have been used in the sociological and anthropological literature to explain generational relationships among kin group and families (Finch, 1989; Finch and Mason, 1993). Husbands, wives, sons, daughters, brothers and sisters have a specific relationship vis-à-vis their responsibility and obligations towards each other. In the body of sociological literature on responsibility and obligations, the adult-child relationship has been described but there is no sociological theory which explains children's domestic work in terms of children's agency and their structural position. Therefore, we need examine the ideas from the literature on family obligations and responsibilities, and apply them to children's domestic work.

Literally, responsibility means a liability towards someone under one's control and authority. Nobody can be held responsible for anything towards anyone who is at the same time not under his or her control or authority. In the context of the domestic sphere Finch and Mason explain family responsibilities as "responsibilities are treated as created commitments rather than rules or obligations ...... they are the product of human agency, and not an external property of social structure over which individuals have no control. ....But there is also a sense in which they become structural features, in that they both constrain and facilitate future actions" (1993:173).

They argue that what each person accumulates over a period of time gives him/her an 'effective' structural position. Explaining their point they point out that if one daughter accumulates wealth while another does not, the result is 'different structural positions' in relation to their parents. There is no dispute over Finch and Mason's (1993) argument but a number of reservations must be noted. We can not apply this as it is in the case of children and childhood responsibilities. Structurally speaking, if childhood is a social category all children carry at least one common group identity: that is of being child. This common group identity is a permanent feature of childhood which exists in all social structures of all times (James *et. al.,*, 1998). This suggests that all children carry at least one common set of responsibilities in any one society. Other set of responsibilities may vary among children of different socio-economic classes in the same society.

It would be interesting to review how the concept of

responsibility has been used in the study of childhood. Under the socialisation paradigm children were thought irresponsible and the training imparted to them was meant to educate them to became responsible adults. The work through which they were trained was always described as instrumental to achieving this end. It was never presented as an indication of their agency as it would then have conflicted with the main notion and the responsibility was deliberately concealed under the weight of obligation. However, some studies have demonstrated how children work as responsible persons in the family (e.g. Seymore 1988, Morrow 1994). We have already referred to Finch and Mason's (1993) argument that responsibilities are the product of human agency. All this suggests that children are responsible actors with a capacity for human agency. The whole perspective of looking at children demands now that the notion of responsibility in respect of children should be explored further so as to explain the full implications of children's agency and their childhood as an integral component of social structure. With the above objective this study uses responsibility and obligation as key concepts in the empirical investigation of children's domestic work.

The second tool is the notion of autonomy and independence. Whether children's work admits of autonomy or not can be ascertained only when we are clear about what we mean by autonomy itself. Let us, therefore, point out the essential ingredients of what we understand by autonomy. An autonomous action presumes that work is done according to free will of the *doer* and is a result of his/her own motive. It is regulated by the doer, critically appraised by him/her and is redolent of responsibility (Dworkin 1989; Benson 1991). There is no literature available, in my knowledge, in which the work of children in a family setting has been examined to see whether it is performed in an autonomous atmosphere or not. So far as I know, only Benson (1991) has touched the issue where he claims that certain forms of socialisation are oppressive and diminish autonomy. His analysis shows how a particular form of socialisation can diminish autonomy. Before this issue, which we will take up later on, the fundamental question is whether a child has or wants autonomy or asserts for autonomy for a social group to which he/she belongs to? It is to be noted here that a debate has already been started in child development studies that children's autonomy should be taken into account. But the theorisation of group autonomy of children is problematic because children have not been recognised as an independent structural category. Once we accept children as an integral and permanent component of society, then it is easy to conceptualise their group autonomy.

To understand children's autonomous agency in terms of their structural position I would like to propose the concept of children's *structural autonomy*. By structural autonomy, I mean that all members of any social structure have some form of freedom for the expression of their agency, which is common to all, and which constitutes their structural autonomy. It helps them in constructing and negotiating their structural relationships with other social structures (e.g. adults, social class, ethnicity etc.). As we know no structure in the society exists in isolation, all are interdependent and inter-related and influence each other. The structural autonomy also works along the principle of interdependence. Interdependence has also been explained in terms of structural interdependence.

There is enough account of research where children's dependent and irresponsible image has been sketched out. In this research the question of children's autonomy does not arise as they are assumed as incompetent and immature. By and large, they are seen to be living in a rigid frame of family structure and school authority. Judged in terms of the ingredients referred to above they have no say on what they are to do, how they are to do it and when they are to do it. They are also accountable to their parents and school teachers. The common conceptualisation is that neither their work is regulated by them nor appraised by them nor they do it with any sense of responsibility. This situation reflects the total neglect of their autonomy and responsible behaviour.

Within the new approach of study of child it has been

found that children do act responsibly (Morrow, 1992) and negotiate their position with adults (Solberg, 1990). So, challenging the notion of irresponsible behaviour and weak position of children in the family, the new approach suggests at least one important fact about children, that children responsibly act and their responsible behaviour leads to interdependency between children and parents in the family (Morrow 1996). With this interdependent social position, children unknowingly or knowingly sometimes affirm their recognition as person.

When children accumulate experiences (of negotiations of life chances) they start asserting for themselves too. This situation normally brings a state of conflict between children's wishes and parents' authority. Parents are conscious of the inevitable break with the past and they are also equally conscious of their continued care for the child. Parents give the impression of treating their children on a different plane, such as a friend, but at the same time they want themselves to be treated as a good and responsible parent (Brannen 1996). Children watch this new situation with caution for it is important for them to know, at this stage, if parents either *want* or *require* them to do the household work. If they want them to report on their activities then there is no conflict but if however they require them to be reported to them peremptorily then children definitely resent it. In this situation, they develop strategies not to report completely or to modify the reports as to retain or increase the limits of their autonomy (Brannen,1996).

Some research has shown how children have been able to negotiate structural autonomy through their work. For example, Solberg's argument is that children "are in a position to influence the outcome of the negotiating process in directions which they perceive to be favourable to themselves" (1990:127). Solberg's data also reveals that children particularly in the family settings start negotiating their position on the basis of their routine work. It clearly makes out a case of the strength of children's agency and contribution to attainment of structural autonomy.

Solberg and Danielsen's (1988) family study shows on the

basis of parental reports on everyday routine work of Norwegian children, that children needed no supervision by adults who have had implicit confidence that child could work independently. This instance shows that in some cases children are appreciated as reliable agents by parents too. Parents, therefore, overlook the consideration of children's age and children are able to secure autonomy through their contribution to work. This suggests that children through their work negotiate their position particularly in age and power structure within the family. How far children succeed in this process remain to be explored.

Our discussion begins with examination of sociological theory relating to children, which indicates that the image of children as agents does not find expression in the beginning. The biologically immature child was weak in all respects. Its incompetence and dependence, institutionalized by both society and social science, stamped out the possibility of agency in the child. Consequently, social scientists refused to take notice of children's work in the family. This elitist perspective regarded them as powerless. The 'becoming' child was looked down upon as 'unbecoming' in all ways. It was an embodiment of all weaknesses and vices. The child was both wild and a threat to society. This was the picture of the child in whom imagining agency was a far cry. The child who could at best only remain submissive to his or her parents could never be thought to be invested with the power of agency. The notions used to describe the child and his presence together make it clear that it was impossible to think of children being at all useful for themselves or for society. The word 'weak' was only a euphemistic word used for children in place of effete. Jenks' (1996) notion of 'absent presence' of the child is a potent pointer to owning abject absence of the agency of the child.

The above discussed conceptualization prevailed in sociological studies well through the 1980s. The new sociological theory, influenced by post-structuralists, shifted the balance in favour of the child. Under this theoretical current, the child-centered approach has emerged with greater clarity and children are considered as a distinct social group. They have begun to be considered as active co-participants of social relationships. Children have been noted as typical, tangible and persistent who participate in society's activities. Like adults, children too interact and affect each other. They are also exposed to the same social events. For example, if family's dissolution affects women, so too does it affect children. Their typical qualities, which are tangibly present in children as a group gives them a permanent structural form. Their innate qualities and interactions with other structural forms like adults give them, in this way, an independent and specific position in the social structure. Their area of activity being confined to domestic space; it is their involvement in domestic work which leads them to their most significant position.

It has been argued that children contribute to the construction of their childhood and society through their work, thus they claim a significant place in the division of labour. Qvortrup's (1985) argument of children's place in the division of labour is justified as there is evidence which show that children's work plays a part in production and re-production of society and its economy. Children materially contribute to the economic structure of society indirectly and to family economy both directly and indirectly. Thus, the place of children's work in the division of labour is indisputable.

An interpretative analysis of children's participative experience of domestic work facilitates the understanding of their contribution to the construction of their own childhood. Children's domestic work forms the basis of children's negotiation with parents and the occasion to set parameters for their participation in work in the future. The form of children's work and the way they realise their agency, shapes their childhood differently from one social class to another.

To sum, the above discussion about children and domestic work rejects the orthodox denial of children's substantial contribution to the domestic work order. By considering the broader definition of work, children's activities in the domestic space are considered as socially meaningful work which is important in the construction of their childhood and to the social order of the family. Nevertheless, a thorough empirical examination by using the concepts such as negotiation, independence, responsibility, obligations etc. is needed to establish the argument.

4

RESEARCHING CHILDREN'S WORK: Methods and Strategies

> Doing research is a messy affair, as dependent on negotiation, adjustment, personal choices and serendipity as on careful and meticulous preparation. ....the distinctions to be made between general methodology, research strategy or procedure and research techniques.
>
> —*James et. al., 1998:169*

Research on children's work in the family largely ignores the views of children. In this research how children interpret their activities is conspicuous by its absence. It has been argued that the prevailing notions of 'incompetency' and 'dependency' were factors which excluded consideration of children as actors in their own right. However, the 'sociology of childhood' regarded children as social actors and viewed their childhood as a socially constructed structure. In this newly emerged approach the research emphasises to take into account children's specific experience of their social life. The importance of children's experience of work, in particular context of their interactions with other structures, has been underlined. In order to understand children's experience of work in the family, the present research tends to contextualise children's agency in the performance of their domestic work, as suggested by Pole and others, 'to recognise its limits and to acknowledge the constraints under which it is realised' (1999:52). Gender and age as structural constraints are, therefore, to be examined in respect of their domestic work and to investigate how far both affect or are affected by work. The examination will expose the limits of their influence. The study reported in this book grew out of the need to fill the gap in sociological understanding regarding children's domestic activities as 'work'. The methods are based on the need to explore children's experiences of work. Since exploring children's point of view forms the basis of data collection, an appropriate methodology was required. The traditional ways of writing research would not always suffice and I took to my own style of writing to enable the reader to know my identity in the context and the reasons why I adopted a particular method or strategy. How research findings can be full of inherent contradictions has been criticised by Stanely and Wise (1983) because of disparity between objectivity and subjectivity. The situation is more complex in the case of research on children where the researcher is an adult. I have been aware of the complexities from the very start of the research. I, therefore, involved children themselves in the interpretation of their experience as and when possible. This device of mine finds support from Morrow and Richards (1996) who have held that children can be involved in interpretation and explanation of their own views.

The Research Setting: Between Coventry and Lucknow

Two specific considerations were involved in selecting the research setting for this study. The first was that it should be the site appropriate to the questions the research seeks to examine and the second was that it should be suitable for qualitative empirical investigation. The considerations therefore included the existence of Indian families carrying on small-scale retailing business and they should have children of the appropriate age group. The final consideration was to find families sharing a common descent but, if possible, living in different sites, so that a comparison could be made and points of contrast may also be examined in addition to the similarities. The potential was to be assessed on the availability of basic requirements and of maximum characteristics of the research subject. The researcher's familiarity with the research site was an important factor in it as children have been noted as "not very used to being asked their opinions and to relate their experiences to unknown adults" (Morrow and Richards, 1996:101).

It may seem curious to situate such a study in Britain and India. Britain, with its multi-racial character, has 5.5 per cent ethnic minorities of which 1.5 per cent are of Indian origin (OPCS, 1991). Research has shown that the cultural tradition of Indian people in Britain, particularly in their community life, has been persistently accommodated in the British socio-economic context (Ballard 1979; James 1974; Jackson and Nesbitt 1993; Nesbitt 1993, 1995; Drury 1991; Bhatti 1994). They are mobilised on cultural grounds. This characteristic feature of the Indian population in Britain brings them together and provides a location for Indians outside India. The practice of cultural traditions, marriage, kinship, practice of religion, ethnic dress and food habits, all have effectively influenced their interactions in social life. By taking a closer look at the children's work in these Indian families I want to explore what social, economic and cultural factors have meant for children and their work. I begin by reviewing what makes Coventry and Lucknow such an interesting case of comparison for the study of children's work in the family.

The choice of Coventry

The demographic and economic characteristics of the Indian population in Coventry have prompted me to select the site for the study. Coventry has an established and relatively well defined population of Indian descent. The ratio of ethnic minorities in Coventry is much higher than in Great Britain as a whole. The percentage of the total population of ethnic minorities in Coventry (i.e. 11.8 percent) is much greater than the average for Great Britain as a whole (i.e. 5.5 percent of the total British population) (Owen, 1995). There were nearly 34,800 people from various ethnic backgrounds living in the city in 1991, of whom 21,600 were of Indian ethnic background. Out these 49 percent were born in the UK and the rest had either migrated directly from the Indian subcontinent or were 'twice migrants'[1] who had moved from countries of East Africa or South East Asia. The age-wise distribution of Coventry's population Census informs us that 8.2 percent of the total child population of the age-group of 0-4 years is of Indian origin. This percentage of Indian children increased to 11.3 percent for the age-group of 5-15 years. However, the number of persons decreases with advancing age. The Indian population in Coventry is relatively young, demographically speaking. This demographic feature suits for the present study.

It is not known when the migration of Indians to Coventry began, however Nesbitt's (1990) study of Valmiki (Indians) has traced it to the mid in 1950's[2]. Most of the Indian immigrants came to Coventry as unskilled labour and were absorbed in the automobile industry during the 1950s and 1960s. The motive of the Indian migrants was economic. Most were young and came as single. As Ballard (1994) puts it, they were 'sojourners rather than settlers'. During the 1960s and 1970s the growth rate of Indian immigrants significantly increased because of family reunion and orientation towards permanent settlement (Ballard 1983; 1990). This growth was further stimulated by the arrival of East African Indian refugees in the 1970s (Bhachu, 1986).

The Indians in Coventry, as in other parts of Britain, are significantly involved in entrepreneurship.[3] Ethnic minorities moved significantly to self-employment and the traditional form of work under waged employment declined. Out of 11.8 per cent of the total ethnic minority population in Coventry 5.4 per cent are engaged in enterpreneurship (Owen, 1995). They usually involved in corner shops, newsagents, groceries, off-licences, retailing of ethnic goods, take-away restaurants, etc. Therefore, Coventry provides me a good location to undertake the study of children's work in Indian families.

The choice of Lucknow

Lucknow is a metropolitan and the capital city of Uttar Pradesh, a state in northern India. Like other metropolitan cities it is also developing fast and attracting people from all over the country. Due to the pressure of population and the absence of heavy industries small business is getting a special impetus. The number of families carrying on small scale business has spread even in the residential areas, just as it has in Coventry. The socio-economic character of the society, especially the middle class, is also undergoing a change. I met there a number of families which combined traditional values with the influence of a modern life style. The children of these families drew my attention as they suited my interest for comparison with Coventry. This is not to say that many other Indian cities did not share the same characteristics. The point is that I was born and brought up in an area of Lucknow which was surrounded by such families in which I had from early childhood established closed connections. My long standing familiarity with the shop owners and their life-style served my purpose. As similar to Coventry, Lucknow also provides me an easy accessibility to the families within the available time and financial resources. Througl. all these considerations Lucknow was chosen as the second site for this research.

General methodological considerations

It has been argued that problems, theory and method in social science are inseparable and are integrated to produce a unique methodology (James and others 1998; Pole *et. al.*, 1999). This can be seen in the theoretical position of the child and the corresponding methods used in childhood research. The earlier theorisation of the children, as muted groups (Hardman, 1973) became a potent factor in the shaping of methodology which took account of the adult's perspective and kept children out of focus during research. The ignorance of children's perspectives to interpret the social relationships and events under the socialisation paradigm constituted a major limitation. The researchers of this position hold that children 'have trouble holding more than one concept at a time in mind. Additionally, their conceptions are limited to ideas that can take concrete, observable forms. They are unable to consider alternative perspectives.... They are just learning how to interpret others' emotions' (Bierman and Schwartz, 1986:268). Due to the invisibility of children's social competence children's views have not been given due importance in understanding their lives. This is why methodologically unifocal research has mostly been done on children but not *with* and *for* them.

In the course of time the concept of children has changed. Charlotte Hardman (1973) was perhaps the first to raise the question of the validity and completeness of childhood research under the socialisation paradigm. In her anthropological research she suggested that "children as people should be studied in their own right" (Hardman 1973: 87). The childhood research has been criticised for its over emphasis on an adult-centric approach where children's voices have been missing (Ambert 1986; Qvortrup 1987; Alanen 1988). The pre-social child is replaced by the pro-social child and s/he is, after reconsideration, regarded as a competent agent. This inclusion of the child's perspective signifies a radical change in the approach to the study of children and childhood. As soon as sociologists start recognising children as social actors, children's views become sociologically important for their study. Children's agencies and competencies have now become a strong methodological tool in recent research (Brannen and O'Brien 1995; Morrow 1992; Mayall 1996). Children's subjective standpoints now become an established element in qualitative research (see e.g. Corsaro 1986; Mandell 1988; O'Brien 1995,

Ulich and Oberhuemer 1992, Laybourn *et. al.*, 1996, Borland *et. al.*, 1998, Pugsley *et. al.*, 1996, Butler and Williamson 1996). Pointing out the advantages of inclusion of children's views James and Prout have suggested that "children are and must be, seen as active in the construction and determination of their own social lives, the lives of those around them and of the societies in which they live" (1990:8).

Qualitative research with children, particularly in family circumstances, has become more significant as it opens new vistas of understandings. Family is the first and foremost ground for children's activities. Children spend most of their time in the family. Therefore, most of their interactions take place within familial circumstances. Children construct and reconstruct their beliefs and views on the basis of their everyday life experiences. Children's beliefs and views eventually shape and define their childhood. So, children's views and experiences in family life are vital to any understanding of their childhood.

A significant gap in the understanding of the degree and nature of children's involvement in domestic work is noticeable even in the literature on domestic work because of the methodology adopted for the study. It does not include children's views. When the degree and nature of children's contribution to domestic work is not reflected fully in research it would be vain to expect any reference to what meaning and significance it has for children.

A question that was raging in my mind for some time past was, if one is not a child should one try to understand what a child's experiences are and can one try to interpret it for others? Thinking this over I came across Goldscheider and Waite's (1991) reference to an incident describing a confidential communication between two reputed sociologists in a session on family change. One whispered into the ear of another, "I have to cook dinner every Thursday and I hate it" (Goldscheider and Waite 1991:1). The suggestion is that whatever the topic men are primarily anxious about their own role in the context. Though every researcher has been a child as s/he comes to write about children s/he just forgets about childhood and slips into an adult frame of mind. It led me to revisit at my own childhood, to know how and where I stood. I wanted to take my bearings in respect of the issue. Can I understand and interpret children's world of experience or have I forgotten all beyond recapturing? Before embarking upon the selection of the topic I wanted to ascertain myself that I had the essential requisites to go ahead. With the experience of my own work as a child could I justify my preference for taking up the domestic work of children as a subject in the first instance? I was born in a middle class Indian family with seven children consisting of two sisters and five brothers. How the interest of the two came into conflict in doing housework, how gender and birth order played an instrumental role in the division of work and how the smart ones amongst us, whether boys or girls outwitted others in performing routine tasks were matters of great interest to me. The traditional norms of the family and the family hierarchy's hold on all of us were understood from the very early stages. Besides the experience of my own family I was also mixing freely with children of other families of the same class which enriched my understanding of various families. Our world, though different from the world of our elders was highly interesting for its variety of incumbents. How orthodoxy and conservatism were constantly being eroded by modernity in our daily lives had its lasting impact on me. The ideas of autocratic rule and unquestioning loyalty were gradually changing. In sharp contrast to my family, some of my friend's families showed the effects of the two set-ups on the children. We had food and clothes to suit our wishes much more easily than they. Similarly in housework too, we enjoyed greater freedom and in between us we experienced better relationships. The ultimate threat of my companion's mother — "my way or high way!" — still keeps ringing in my ears and reminds me how coercive and cruel parents can be in some cases.

It has been noticed that biographical experiences help to establish rapport with respondents and are helpful in understanding the social relationships in different social settings (Hammersley and Atkinson 1995). My biographical experiences also enabled me to utilise past experience in gaining access to children themselves. The fact that I was an Indian and was conversant with Indian socio-cultural values prompted me to take up the study of Indian children in Coventry where I was placed. Just as Hughes' (1992) and Blackman's (1995) biographical factors played a vital role in gaining relevant information during their respective research on step-families and youth culture, my status also enabled me to get optimum access to Indian families, short of insider status, which was a special priviledge accruing to me particularly in Coventry.

On the basis of prerequisites for qualitative research and of my own experience with the pilot interviews, I decided to concentrate on detail rather than on the quantity of data by working with a small number of children. During the pilot interviews, I calculated that at least three weeks were necessary for the study of each family. The time factor was also an important consideration for sticking on a small sample size. After deciding a small sample size for the study I was interested in exploring the most suitable age-group of children for this study. Although Solberg (1990) has strongly argued that age should be ignored in drawing children's perspectives on their work, I decided to include boys and girls between 10 to 15 years. This is because of two main reasons. Firstly, it is suggested that children of this age group are the most potential source of information. Amato and Ochiltree (1987), for example, found that the data available from children aged between 8 to 9 years is relatively less qualitative than that of the children aged between 15-16. Oakley and others (1995) also argue that younger children (i.e., 5-8 years) will rarely give reliable data for the purpose of research, and this is also supported by McGurk and Glachan (1988) in their study of children's conversation with adults. They found that young children took longer to respond to sensitive issues; moreover sometimes they take the perceptions of adults (especially their parents) into account on such matters. Secondly, the existing studies found that children of the age-group of 10-15 contribute substantially to housework. For example, White and Brinkerhoff (1981) find that 'by the age of 9 or 10 well over 90 per cent are involved in regular chores'; Zill and Peterson's (1982) study find that in the sample of children of 7-11 years, children of 9-11 years are especially marked for undertaking maximum household activities. While I was not disputing the fact that children of younger age group may produce reliable data (which is demonstrated in the research undertaken by Corsaro *et. al.*, (1986) and Mayall (1996)) and may contribute to housework, I decided to study children of age-group 10 -15 in order to steer clear of the practical difficulties in understanding the younger group and to maximise the data on children's experience of work.

Once I decided the small size of sample from a particular age-group, the question of selecting the sample was crucial for me. I decided to select the sample through a snowball sampling procedure. This approach, according to Burgess, "involves using a small group of informants who are asked to put the researcher in touch with their friends who are subsequently interviewed, then asking them about their friends and interviewing them until a chain of informants has been selected" (1990: 55). I found this method of sampling most suitable to my this study because an adequate frame of sampling was not available. This sampling procedure also suited to this study as I was concerned with only a specific type of families that is families of Indian descent who run the corner shops in Coventry and Lucknow. Because of the specific characteristics of the sample, this sampling procedure was found most suitable for the study.

Having made these decisions, I approached fifteen families who were running their own corner shops/newsagent shops in both Coventry and Lucknow by taking introductory note from one family to other. Since corner shops/ new agent shop owners of Indian origin were tend to know about each other it was easier for me to approach 15 families in both the cities. Out of these fifteen families I selected only ten families in both the places. In total twenty families I interviewed 41 children in out of which 24 were girls and 17 were boys. The data was collected during the winters of the year1998.

To understand children's lives and their 'limited social

experience' in-depth interviews are the most favoured technique within the sociology of childhood (James *et. al.*, 1998). In-depth interviews itself recognises children as persons in their own right. As persons their competency has been displayed through their active participation in qualitative interviews (Siegert, 1986). Use of children's subjective explanations of various issues in sociological analysis has changed the direction of the debate. Children's competency in conversation with adults provided an opportunity to challenge the long standing concept of 'dependency' in childhood (Morrow1992). Children's competency in explaining their experiences not only provide strong evidence for proving their agency but also show their ability in self-expression. Thus, interviewing children provides an appropriate vehicle for gaining access to their experiences and understanding of their social worlds.

Another reason for considering qualitative interviews as a tool for data collection was the nature of this study. The main purpose of this study was to explore children's account of their daily lives in the family and therefore participant observation was difficult, given that children do housework at unfixed hours. It was not possible for me to stay on for long with them. The access to and adjustment with family settings for long periods was also practically very difficult. Therefore, appropriateness of interview method and considering the demands of the present study, I decided to use focused and in-depth interviews. For this purpose I used an interview guide which was carefully prepared. It covered all the pertinent topics of enquiry related to the research issue. The topics included were children's extent and nature of domestic work, its meaning and significance, age and gender of children and their domestic work besides the socio- personal profile of the respondents. The information obtained by one child was used in interviewing the other child. This technique not only helped me to draw rich information from children, but also gave me a chance to familiarise myself with the children, so facilitating a purposeful conversation. May (1993) is also of the opinion that the collection of information with the help of unstructured interview provides qualitative depth in the research process. The unstructured interviews in an informal atmosphere also allowed the children to raise the issues important to them in the ways that they wanted. The interviews with children were conducted on an individual basis. The pilot study established that the family could provide more information through individual interviews than group interviews. Group interviews are suggested as a useful technique mostly in school settings where a number of children are available at one place, but in family settings where they are fewer in number, I found individual interview to be a more useful device for collecting data.

Children had to be approached with extreme caution and consideration. To take them into confidence the interview technique had to be modified and refined from time to time. Peering into their home life, having an intimate glimpse of their worlds of work and their interactions with parents, called for sensitivity and care. Following Butler and Williamson's (1994) advice the intention was to allow the children a degree of choice in — where to be interviewed, how to be interviewed, when to be interviewed and whether they wished to be recorded. On occasion, the strategies of interview had to be changed. Sometimes parental proximity was helpful while at other times it was a serious stumbling block to frank and spontaneous conversation. In those situations where parents were past masters in contriving situations, engineering facts and even conniving with children they had to be kept away discreetly. In some cases, the muzzled information on housework could only be frankly discussed in the absence of parents. Ferreting out details that could be dependable, therefore, warranted extreme care and caution and devising of indirect ways to merit examination.

To create such a situation where children could reveal their real experiences often became the crux of the practical problems for me. One can think that either children are quite closely related to their parents or they have very little connection with them. But in my experience the truth lies in between these two extremes. It would be simplistic to hold that all people are transparent and their motives are self-evident. Parents' stress on strict discipline and on the total subservience of their children on the pretext of the best interest of the child savours, at times, of exploitation and the abuse of autocratic power. The ambivalent nature of parents, therefore, requires that they should not be taken for granted. The series of interviews conducted have borne out this fact, for even a slight scratching of the surface of their inter-communication has divulged alarming incidents of shrewd patterns of coercion and masterly machinations. The sweep of children's experience in relation to their domestic work was simply astonishing. With the odds of theoretical bias and family circumstances stacked against them, getting down to their personal experience has been a very trying and difficult job. The unknown and the unsuspected have often appeared in staggering steps. Even the thumbnail sketch of an idea or event by children had much to reveal about their reaction to relationships and their attitude to work. This could be expected only in an atmosphere of free give and take with no hangovers of any sorts.

I had never thought that the researcher's gender in researching children would appear in the way it did during my encounter with children. I found that parents who were apprehensive that their children may not inadvertently reveal their business or home secrets became more trusting when my wife accompanied me. Her presence served as a sort of assurance and parents who otherwise were in the habit of dropping in during sessions much felt relieved by enquiring from her how it was progressing. I also found that some girls were withdrawn, reticent and shy at times in my presence. Even after my best efforts to persuade them to speak their responses were often monosyllabic. My own gender was the chief handicap in communication and made me a *de trop* to children. I therefore enlisted the help of my wife since she had experience of working with children. The girls always thawed with the appearance of one of their own sex, opened up and became more vocal. The role of gender in researching the children dawned upon me in a memorable way. She was instrumental not only in gaining access to children but also in making the communication meaningful.

Lastly I took precautions that my adult perception may not distort the interpretation and significance of children's version. For this I resorted to the practice of putting their views to the next child interviewed for confirmation or otherwise of the meaning. Ennews and Morrow's (1994) advice 'if you don't know what a child is trying to depict ask another child!' validates the strategy I evolved to get one child's version interpreted by another, whenever possible. All of these steps were taken, of course, in addition to my attempt to sound *minimally adult* and to *maximise* children's participation through the entire period of interaction.

Some ethical considerations in childhood research in family settings

Although the professional bodies (e.g. British Sociological Association and Association of Social Anthropologists) have formulated a general code of conduct on ethics in social research, there are no specific ethical considerations for researching children. However, the recent childhood research and agencies concerned with children's rights (e.g. National Children's Bureau) have initiated discussions on the ethical issues involved. The theoretical and empirical studies have raised, and subsequently tried to resolve, many issues in researching children. Fine and Sandstorm's (1988) 'Knowing Children' and Alderson's (1995) 'Listening to Children' raises some ethical concerns pertinent to this research. Some of the psychologists and medical researchers have also contributed in this discussion.

A key ethical issue involved in childhood research is linked to children's current social status, particularly in the industrialised world (James *et. al.*, 1998). Some child researchers (Morrow and Richards 1996; Lansdown 1994) observe that the current social image of children has a direct bearing on childhood research. They believe that the socially constructed vulnerability and powerlessness of children in the modern world legitimises parents' plea to protect their children. The protective, and sometimes over-protective, relationship lessens the children's participation in the research process too. Butler and Williamson (1994) are of the opinion that gatekeepers become barriers to children's participation. So, the children's vulnerable and weak social status creates a situation which is very peculiar, particularly for research. In a situation where a researcher holds a child development perspective, there is less possibility of complications. In this situation both the gatekeepers' and researchers' adult-centric views coalesce and for this reasons access becomes relatively easier. However, there is a possibility that children's views do not come out freely in this situation. On the other hand, when a researcher holds a child-centred perspective in which s/he wants to use children's views and life-experiences, access to children becomes more complicated. In this situation the imbalance in power and status between the child and the adult becomes more apparent. This situation has been described by Morrow and Richards as, 'the biggest challenge' (1996:98). As suggested by Thomas and O'Kane (1998) this challenge could be to "redress the power imbalance between child participant and adult researcher, in order to enable children to participate on their own terms" (1998:337).

Noting the challenge of the power relationship between the adult and the child in the process of research, some authors have suggested three main areas where a careful consideration of research ethics is required (e.g. Fine and Sandstrom, 1988; Morrow and Richards, 1996; Thomas and O'Kane, 1998). These areas are consent, confidentiality or privacy and protection. On the basis of recently laid down guidelines and suggestions in the literature on childhood research, and my own practical experience of interviewing children for the pilot study, I resolved these ethical issues in my field work for the this study.

Informed Consent

It is ethically very important for a researcher to have the

child's consent before getting involved in the research process. Where research subjects are children, gaining consent is rather difficult and complex. This is the case because children's world of understanding normally differs from that of adults. The difference between the two makes gaining the child's trust difficult and without trust in the research relationship a researcher cannot gain the child's consent. Therefore, gaining the trust of the child is one of the fundamental requirements of research. Butler and Williamson's (1994) study explains the difficulties in gaining this trust. They suggest that research on sensitive and controversial issues with children demands special care in handling. By providing relevant and necessary information with adequate assurance of protection a researcher can earn the trust of children that could be helpful in gaining their consent.

The consent gaining process is complex in child research as it involves two stages. In family circumstances, Mahon and others (1996) make it clear that initially the researcher has to take the parents formal permission to talk to their children. The children's consent is to be taken independently. It might simultaneously happen that children may or may not agree to an interview. While in educational settings (e.g. school) the gate-keepers are teachers, head teachers and/or other school authorities, and a researcher has to take formal permission of them, it has been noted by Mauthner (1997) that getting access to children in the family is more complicated than in the school. In both settings the researcher is supposed to explain his/her purpose and the objective of the study to adults before gaining the children's consent. After gaining adults' consent, children's consent is then to be established. In this way the whole process becomes complex.

In fact, there are two views about the necessity of the respondent's consent. One view holds that gaining the consent of the respondent is relatively important, while another view holds the informed consent of the interviewee before the interview to be of foremost importance (see e.g. Burger 1984; 1988; Mahon *et. al.*, 1996; Hill *et. al.*, 1996). Fontana and Frey

(1994), advocate that consent should be received from the respondents after explaining carefully and truthfully the objectives and purpose of the research. There is a dispute regarding how much a researcher should tell about the object of the study to gain the consent of the subjects. On this issue, Morrow and Richards' (1996) suggestion that researcher choices are always open in order to respond to a particular situation is very relevant. I have used this as a solution to resolve the dilemma and explained the objectives of my research to children and their parents. I told them only as much as I felt was necessary to gain their consent and trust.

I have obtained the informed consent of parents as well as children for the interviews, as this was necessary for access to the children. Here, my personal (Indian) background was very helpful, since I arranged a formal meeting with parents and introduced myself to the whole family. As regards the research project, I explained them about the aim and scope of the interviews with their children. I was very careful about using the negative notion of 'child labour' as commonly understood while explaining about children's 'work' and 'activities'. Therefore, I deliberately avoided the phrase 'child labour' and used 'child's work' or 'child's job' or 'child's activities' during conversation. After providing satisfactory information, in the first stage, I asked for formal permission to contact the children and afterwards in the following meeting I asked for the children's consent. Morrow and Richards (1996) observe that children, sometimes, may want to dissent, but because of family and obligations, do not feel free to do this. In my research I gave children freedom to either decline or postpone the interviews. Mahon *et. al.*, also pointed out that children "may have regarded the interviewer as an authority figure or succumbed to parental pressure to participate in the research process" (1996:151). So, to avoid unwilling or forced participation, I spent considerable time ensuring the children had chosen freely to participate. Most of the time, I established their consent in the absence of other family members. I was mostly successful in gaining their trust. My wife's knack of striking a chord with children ultimately helped me in persuading the girl to be interviewed. This experience made me realise that only when a child becomes familiar with a researcher's objective can his/her conversation become more fruitful. Contrary to this experience, in Lucknow, I found it easy to converse with children because of their enthusiasm for a rare opportunity to express their own views to an outsider particularly on family issues. All were quite willing to take part in the discussion and never refused to talk. This might have happened because the arrangements were usually made by their parents.

Confidentiality

Ethics play a significant role in building rapport. In the process of gaining trust a researcher has to assure the respondent about the confidentiality of the data. Burgess (1988) very rightly raises the question: to what extent do people expose the private aspects of their lives? He called it an 'invasion of privacy'. The extent of 'invasion of privacy' is also a matter of serious ethical concern while talking to adults but it becomes more complex in research with children. In researching children it becomes a very sensitive issue as it may happen that the researcher's invasive questions suffer from the risk of abusing children due to their lack of knowledge and/or lack of power of expression. This risk factor is very significant. For this purpose, researchers are advised to assure maximum confidentiality and privacy regarding the responses, views and beliefs and to the use of pseudonyms (Burgess, 1988).

To consider the seriousness and sensitivity of this factor, I guaranteed the maximum confidentiality of responses and the use pseudonyms to hide children's real identity. In my experience I found that children both in Coventry and in Lucknow were unconcerned about confidentiality. It is interesting to note that Lucknow children even questioned the use of pseudonyms. They wanted to be named along with their views. Some of the Coventry children also wished the same.

But following the ethical guidelines referred to earlier I emphasised the importance of not using their real names. About the confidentiality of their statements, most of them were bold enough to share their views openly. It may be the case that they were getting a rare opportunity to express themselves and took the opportunity eagerly.

Protection

The third and very significant ethical issue for consideration is children's protection from physical, emotional or any other kind of harm during research and afterwards (Fontana and Frey, 1995). During the course of investigation, the protection of respondents is the responsibility of the researcher. In medical research, the probability of physical harm is greater, whilst in researching children about their family, it may happen that the respondent may become emotionally hurt by some questions. Therefore, the research ethics lay down that a researcher should not ask very direct and hurtful questions to children regarding sensitive issues. For example children in single parent families should be interviewed very carefully in respect of their experience with family members.

Alderson (1995) suggests that research with children should be examined in terms of its 'impact on children'. According to her, the confidentiality should be maintained about the research subjects as much as possible because it may have an impact when the children grow up. The disclosure of identity and data may harm these children in the future. Therefore, in research with children, these issues should be undertaken very carefully.

On the basis of suggestions made for the protection of children's interests during the research process, I have taken great care and caution in the interview process. I did not ask direct questions which could hurt children's feeling on issues such as the division of domestic labour; inequality in the distribution of housework and parental pressure for housework. Although I have inquired about these issues during my investigation I have protected their emotional feelings on such sensitive issues.

NOTES

1. Many Indians who had settled in East Africa (Kenya, Uganda and Tanzania in particular) were forced to leave these countries during the early 1970s. Britain was a natural choice to settle as many held British passports. See Bhachu (1985).
2. Nesbitt (1990, 1995) traced the early migration of Indians in Coventry. She refers to Peter Khalas's (Coventry Reminiscence Theatre 1990:59-61) claim that the arrival of the first four Indians in Coventry took place in 1935. However, most Indian settlers came to Coventry from the 1950s onwards.
3. In official publications entrepreneurs are described as economically active people who are self-employed with employees or small scale business people. See Owen (1995).

5

THE NATURE AND THE EXTENT OF CHILDREN'S WORK IN THE FAMILY

For reconsideration of children's work we need to look at two issues: how we theoretically conceive 'the child'? And the how we see an activity as 'work'? As far as children's theoretical position is concerned I believe that this matters significantly decisive, at least, for considering children's activities as 'work'. Since children were regarded as 'incompetent' and 'irresponsible', their activities were seen either as a source of their cognitive, emotional, and social development (see Goodnow 1988) or as a role-rehearsal for future life (White and Brinkerhoff 1981; Thrall 1978). In fact, the image of children as incompetent and irresponsible prevents researchers from seeing their activities as 'work' involving competent and responsible persons. However, if we theoretically accept that children are persons in their own right, the interpretation changes. This is exemplified in Virginia Morrow's (1992, 1996) study of children's work where she has theoretically accepted children as actors of their own right. On the basis of empirical evidence, she argues that children contribute to the domestic economy through their domestic work, which was earlier unrecognised. I will be examining children's domestic activities within the theoretical position which I had proposed in the previous chapter. I have also rejected the conventional definition of work under which children's domestic activities were not duly recognised as 'work'. Within the extended definition of work, an activity is to be regarded as 'work', if it is organised against the labour demand, constitutes a permanent part of the work order, involves the conversion of ideas, material and resources and affects or affected by the social relationship. Here I would like to analyse children's domestic activities in order to understand how far they resemble to 'work' which contribute to the maintenance of the domestic work order.

In the following paragraphs a close examination of the extent and types of children's domestic activities has been done. Children's activities can be classified into five different categories: self-provisioning, house-maintenance, kitchen work, caring and miscellaneous activities. The examination reveals that children's domestic activities in both Coventry and Lucknow are quite substantial and vital for the functioning of the family. It has been argued that children's self-provisioning activities, which are generally overlooked in the discussion of children's housework, are important constituent of domestic labour since they significantly affect others, particularly mothers. My next step is to examine the nature of these activities in the light of the prevailing definition of work. Four main features of children's domestic activities have been identified: the organised response of labour demand; the permanent recurrence of these activities; the management of time and skills involved in these activities; and its economic value for the family. On the basis of these features the chapter argues in the last section that children's activities are, in all fairness of the scope of the definition of work, 'work' and substantially contribute to the domestic work order.

SECTION I

THE TYPE AND THE EXTENT OF CHILDREN'S DOMESTIC ACTIVITIES

Children's Self-Provisioning Jobs

Children in both Coventry and Lucknow reported that they carry out a number of tasks in their routine. Children carry out some of the tasks such as making their own bed, getting dressed, tidying up their rooms, washing and ironing the clothes, arranging their school bag, laying the table for breakfast and meals for themselves, while caring for siblings, tidying up the whole house, cooking meal for the family and washing dishes are the jobs which they undertake for the family. Because some of the children's routine tasks primarily serve the purpose of their own provisioning, we categorise them as the *'self-provisioning'* activities. These activities have already been identified as involving 'self-care' (Goodnow and Delaney 1989, Brannen 1995) or 'self-maintenance' (Morrow 1992) activities. However, the analysis of these activities so far is focused on children themselves, but not on others. For instance, Goodnow and Delaney (1989) have compared children's 'self-care' activities with their 'family-care' activities and argued that children's 'self-care' activities are vital for their socialization. They found that the mothers in the study regarded this category of activity as children's work; and that mothers supervised them where children failed to carry out their self-care. Although Mayall (1996) has touched upon the importance of children's self-provisioning activities, particularly in the maintenance of health-order in the family, but no other author has regarded it as component of the division of domestic labour.

Interestingly, all those activities which children perform for themselves are not generally considered as 'work', but they do become 'work' when carried out by mothers. Perhaps, this is a consequence of the different contexts under which these activities have been performed. When a mother performs 'child-care' it is assumed that she contributes to the maintenance of the family, yet when a child undertakes 'self-provisioning' tasks it is considered that these are for their own benefit. The question to be asked is: are children's self-provisioning activities only useful for themselves? or Do children's self-provisioning activities affect other members of the family? Answers to these questions can only be ascertained if children's self-provisioning activities are seen in the context of the social order of the family. The important point here is that those activities which children perform for the provision of their families are identified as 'family-care' activities and regarded as 'housework' by some researchers (Goodnow and Delaney 1989, Brannen 1995, Morrow 1992), while those activities which children perform for their self-provision, are left unexamined. Thus, to remove this ambiguity in the understanding of children's self-provisioning activities we need to examine these activities in the context of the family.

A closer examination of children's accounts in the present study reveals that children self-provisioning activities relieve their parents from child-care. By undertaking the responsibility of self-provisioning children reduce the burden of housework of parents. For instance, Rekha (Lucknow, 13, F) explains:

Rekha: I have been doing my jobs for the last six or seven years. I do all my jobs by my own.

Sometimes my mummy helps me in washing my clothes..... but she never makes my bed, tidies up my room or keeps my school uniform. These things normally I do because she [mummy] says that everyone should do their own work......

VC: When you were young who was doing these jobs?

Rekha: When I was young she [mother] was doing all this for me...... like washing and ironing my school uniform, preparing my school lunch but when I was eight she stopped doing these jobs. She asked me to do my own work. And from then I started doing my jobs.

VC: What does your mummy do now?

Rekha: She does a lot of other jobs. She looks after the whole family. She helps my papa [father] in the shop.........

Viv (Coventry, 10, M) says:

Viv: I normally do all my job....... (I) tidy-up my room, tidy my clothes, polish my shoes, make bed, sometimes clear the mess in my room.

VC: When did you start doing these jobs?

Viv: Since seven.

VC: Who was doing this job before you?

Viv: My mum and Roop [sister].

VC: Why have they given it to you?

Viv: My mum works in the shop and she doesn't get time. She's got too many jobs to do ...... and Roop [sister] is busy with her college. Well.... she [Roop] has other jobs as well.... (like) she cooks, cleans, and washes. So I do my jobs. Even sometimes I help them [mother and sister] in cleaning.

Hari (Coventry, 12, M) reports:

VC: What is your normal routine?

Hari: ...I wake up at about seven and brush my teeth and then go to toilet and get fresh. Then I set my school bag and pack my lunch. I have my breakfast and then go to school. I come back at nearly half past three and have something to eat. I play and watch telly for a while and then stay in the shop. In the evening I study for an hour and tidy up my room, and my clothes. I pull up my bed. Sometimes I set the table for dinner, wipe up and whatever ......and then go to bed. That's it.

VC: What about weekends?

Hari: Saturdays I get up very late........about at ten or so. I do some cleaning and watch telly. Put my clothes for washing. Then I have dinner. I play for sometime. Sometimes I go to my cousin's house too. In the evening I usually sit in the shop and then again watch telly and go to bed. .... Sundays are like Saturdays. I get up late. Normally Sundays are very hectic because we have to do hoovering, dusting and cleaning of all house. Sometimes we have guests on Sundays. My mum oes cooking for them. We have to wash clothes and dry them up and iron them on Sundays. Sometimes we also go out on Sundays.

VC: O.k....... it seems that you do your jobs. Do you?

Hari: Yes, I do.

VC: How long you have been doing these jobs?

Hari: When I was six.

VC: Why do you do these jobs?

Hari: If we don't then who will do it. This is our job.

VC: Could you tell me an experience when you did not do your work.

Hari: Usually I do my work but whenever I don't do it then my mum does. My mum doesn't like doing it and gets upset. She always says "you are big enough to do your work and everyone should do his work". In fact she has so many other jobs to do. Look, if she takes care of me then how she'll get time to do other things.

Like Hari, there are many other children in this study who revealed that when they reached at the age of six and/or seven they began to undertaken responsibility of their own care. In this way, children's involvement in self-provisioning activities is a direct transfer of 'child-care' from the parent , usually a mother, to a child. By way of transferring 'child-care' to children themselves parents are relieved. There is evidence that parents use the time which they save from the child-care to carry out other jobs. For instance, Viv recalled in above quote that his mother did all his job when he was young, but when he took on greater responsibility for his own jobs, his mother increased her contribution to the family business. It is clear from this perspective that children's involvement in their own self-provisioning, particularly in Coventry, provides an opportunity for parents to become more involved in the family business, as mothers in particular become available to contribute more labour. This therefore suggests that children's self-provisioning activities affect the degree of participation of mothers in the labour force.

Another important feature which we have noticed is that children's self-provisioning activities constitute an essential part of the domestic work order. It has been noticed that if children fail to perform their self-provisioning according to the family's established standards, the domestic work order gets disturbed. Children are expected to discharge their responsibilities of self-care in an approved manner. For example, Hari's quote illustrates that if a child fails to carry out thier self-provisioning jobs its impact on parents is considerable. In such case, parents (especially mothers) have to step in and save the domestic work order from being upset. Like Hari, few other children reported that any change in children's self-provisioning activities brings disorder to family arrangements. Normally children have less choice in the way they perform the self-provisioning activities. In some cases, if they have been found carrying out a job which is against expected patterns of behaviour parents step in to correct them. It is not only a question of how a child behaves, but also how he/she performs their self-provisioning activities. Rekha (Lucknow, 13, F) explains:

Rekha: My mummy doesn't like me to mess. She wants everything to be in the drawer or on the shelf.

Whenever I leave the things on bed or on the table she asks me to do it as she wants. Sometimes I follow her but sometimes I argue with her that this is my table and my room ...... why ain't I allowed to keep my things as I want? But mummy says that it doesn't look proper. She always expect me to put them in a drawer. Normally I have no other way to put them but have to put them as she wants.

VC: If you fail to do this then what happens?

Rekha: Then she becomes annoyed. Sometimes she does it for me but warns me for the next time.

Rahul (Lucknow, 14,M) described how he was strategically involved in self-provisioning jobs:

Rahul: My mummy says that you have to clean your room. "It doesn't matter whether you like it or not, cleaning has to be done".

VC: If you don't do it, then what happens?

Rahul: Then she tells to my papa [father]. What else then? We have to do all the jobs what she wants to be done.

Ravi (Coventry,12, M) recounts his experience as follows:

Ravi: Whenever I put my clothes on the bed my mum shouts at me to put them in the wardrobe. She says "don't put clothes everywhere". Sometimes I put them in a laundry basket but sometimes I leave them as it is.

VC: How does your mum react to it?

Ravi: She never allows me to leave my clothes on the bed. She wants me to do everything in order and I have to listen her. I do whatever she wants. I tidy up my room, my table, clear the mess in my room, make my bed.

VC: Do you enjoy the jobs?

Ravi: Yes I do, but not always. She [mother] always wants the jobs to be done as she wants which upsets me.

VC: Why?

Ravi: Because I don't understand it ..... if the room is mine then why aren't I allowed to keep it as I want. Why they [parents] interfere in it. It's not fair.

The above examples clearly show how these children carry out their self-provisioning activities. They perform their activities in a well-controlled and regulated atmosphere. If children do not perform the self-care activities then parents use certain strategies (e.g. appreciation, monetary rewards, denial or sanction of privileges) to maintain the established order of caring or provisioning (Gill 1998). The evidence also shows that few children object to parent's expectation in this area. For example, both Ravi and Rahul objected to their parents' demand to tidy up their rooms since both felt that this was none of their parents concern. Both felt they should be allowed to keep their room as they preferred. But the fact is that the standard presumed in 'family-care' is maintained as such for 'self-care' too, irrespective of the agent which could be either parents or children. Children are not permitted to allow the family's standard to suffer. Every family saw to it that their children not only behave as expected, but that they should also dress according to family customs. The self-provisioning activities are fully influenced by family practices and performed in accordance with them. Furthermore, it follows that a child has consciously to put in mental and physical effort to act according to these expectations.

What is important to note here is that children's self-provisioning activities, both in Coventry and Lucknow, affect not only their lives, but also significantly affect the work order of the family. The findings about children's self-provisioning activities are: firstly, children's activities related to their self-care are a direct transfer of domestic chores from mothers to children on a permanent basis; secondly, it reduces parents' responsibility of child-care; thirdly, it frees parents to undertake other jobs (e.g. mothers find more time to work in family business); and lastly, these activities are undertaken in a regulated atmosphere and, therefore, are not spontaneous activities such as leisure or play. Importantly, the variation in social contexts of Indian children in both Coventry and Lucknow does not show any significant difference. These findings lead us to recognise them as part of the domestic work order in general and suggests the need to consider them, in all fairness, as children's 'work'. The significance of children's self-provisioning activities in terms of their contribution to domestic work will be considered in greater detail in the next chapter.

Children's House-maintenance Jobs

House-maintenance is the most common area in which children of both Coventry and Lucknow are found to be greatly involved. Children carry out cleaning, dusting, sweeping, mopping, vacuum cleaning, tidying the house as part of their routine. Besides these jobs they also help in the laundry, grocery shopping and gardening. Since the purpose of these activities is to maintain the house, we call them 'house-maintenance' jobs. Although the study finds that children in both places were involved in house-maintenance jobs, the extent of children's involvement significantly varies between Coventry and Lucknow. The main reason for the variation is the difference in their socio-economic set-up. The study found that the demand of labour is greater and the availability of domestic appliances is less in Lucknow for maintenance of the house, which amounts to greater involvement of Lucknow children in house-maintenance jobs than that of Coventry children. For example the environmental conditions in Lucknow are such that the houses become more dusty than in Coventry. Because of the dust, sweeping and dusting in Lucknow houses, both at sunrise and sunset, is unavoidable. Domestic technology is not generally affordable and, therefore, the use of a vacuum cleaner is not common. All the cleaning jobs are done manually thus requiring greater time and energy. Due to the excessive demand of labour, some of the Lucknow families have employed maid servants for sweeping and mopping. On asking about the daily routine, Puja, a 14 year old Lucknow girl reports:

Puja: Today? Yeah!... I swept the rooms in the morning. Then I made morning tea for everybody. After serving tea to mummy and papa I had bath and then I got dressed for school. I ate my breakfast and then I went to school. After coming back from school I had my meals and came to the shop for some time. Then you have arrived. That is it (laugh)...

VC: What will you do when I will leave?

Puja: I have to sweep and dust the room. Then I have to do some work in the kitchen. I will do all that jobs till seven (in the evening). From seven to eight I normally watch television and then I have to do my school homework. I will take my dinner at nine and then again I will watch television for some time or I will study. Then I will go to bed.

VC: Is this your daily routine?

Puja: Yes it is. Normally I don't do sweeping in the morning. But from the last two days my maid servant is not coming, so I have to do it. But when she will be back I'll not do it. I do everything in the evening.

VC: What about the Sunday?

Puja: On Sundays I have more jobs to do. I do cleaning, mopping, washing the clothes, and cooking the meals.

VC: How much time do you spend on these jobs on Sundays?

Puja: More than half day. Usually I will finish the jobs by two o'clock in the afternoon. If somebody visits us then it may take longer.

VC: And what about weekdays?

Puja: Normally, it takes me about an hour in the morning

and about two to three hours in the evening. But it's not fixed. Sometimes It takes me less and sometimes more. It all depends, if there are many jobs I have to spend more time to wind it up.

Like Puja, Radha (Lucknow, 14, F) reveals the extent of her involvement in house maintenance jobs:

Radha: I do almost the cleaning jobs.

VC: Like what?

*Radha:*Like sweeping, mopping, dusting, tidying up the lounge.

VC: How much time do you give to these jobs?

Radha: Everyday I do sweeping and dusting in the evening. It takes me about one and half hour to finish this. Then I do a bit of tiding up that takes about half an hour.

VC: Do you do the same on Sundays?

Radha: Oh! No Sunday is very hectic for me. Because I have to clean the house both in the morning and in the evening. There are always some visitors on Sundays so I have to arrange the sitting room nicely and tidy up the whole house as well. All this takes my three to four hours. That's really boring.

Both the above quotes suggest that these girls spend about twenty to twenty five hours per week on house-maintenance jobs whereas in Coventry, girls reported spending about ten hours per week. The reason why it takes less time for house-maintenance jobs in Coventry is that the girls use vacuum cleaners which save both time and energy. It is also evident that Coventry girls do vacuum cleaning only once in a week. It is evident in Roop's (Coventry, 15, F) statement:

Roop: Normally I do dusting, tidying up and hoovering. On week days I tidy up the house and do a bit of dusting because I don't get much time. But on weekends I hoover the whole house.

VC: How much time do you give for these jobs?

Roop: On week days it takes me about an hour to do all the cleaning jobs. But in weekends I spend more time on it. For hoovering, dusting and tiding up it takes about three hours.

Further to be noted that in Coventry, boys were found to be less involved in these jobs in comparison to girls and in

Lucknow, boys' contribution to jobs like sweeping and mopping was negligible; although they did undertake grocery shopping and gardening jobs. This suggests that there is a distinctive gender-typing of children's house-maintenance jobs. Its implications for children will be discussed in the next chapters.

Children's Kitchen Work

Children, particularly girls, were found to be involved in kitchen work. Both in Coventry and Lucknow children reported that they undertake most of the tasks normally carried out by their mothers. This includes the preparation and cooking of meals, serving, washing-up, and managing the left-over food for reuse. All types of kitchen work constitute a major portion of the domestic work order in these families. Both mothers and girls are found to be sharing kitchen work, although girls in Lucknow normally spend more time than those in Coventry. For example, Smriti (Lucknow, 15, F) describes:

Smriti: I and my mummy cook food for all. ....I start processing vegetables for curry at six in the evening. Then my mummy makes curry. Later on I make chapatis and serve food to everybody. Sometimes I make *dal* in the evening. I love making it.

VC: How much time do you spend in cooking?

Smriti: About two hours everyday. But sometimes it is more when there are some guests expected. We have to make special dishes.

However, Leena (Coventry, 13, F) reports:

Leena: I cook almost every evening. I love making curry and dal. But I hate making rotti [chapati]. So my mum makes it.

VC: How much time do you take in cooking?

Leena: Just about an hour.

VC: Who washes dishes?

Leena: In the evening I wash dishes but in the morning my mum does.

VC: How much time it takes in washing up the dishes?

Leena: About half an hour.

In the above two quotes it is evident that the girl from Lucknow is spending more time in the kitchen than the Coventry girl. There were other similar examples found in both Coventry and Lucknow which suggest that girls' involvement in Lucknow in kitchen work is relatively more than that in Coventry. The noticeable reason of this difference is that Coventry families use modern kitchen appliances and processed and/or half-processed food material more frequently. However, families in Lucknow do not use modern domestic appliances such as four burner cooker, microwave oven, grill, electric mixer and grinder, electric toaster, etc. Processed or half-processed food is also not popular in Lucknow. In such circumstances the processing of food material and cooking of meals take more time in Lucknow than that in Coventry. Consequently, children have to put more time in kitchen work.

It is further noted that there is a difference in the involvement of boys and girls in both Coventry and Lucknow, which suggests that the child's gender is an important variable for the involvement in kitchen work. The children's experience of gender in kitchen work and its implications for their childhood will be discussed in greater detail in next chapter.

Children's caring activities

Unlike, in house-maintenance and kitchen work, children in Coventry were found to be more involved in caring activities when compared to the Lucknow children. Some children still care for siblings while some had cared for their siblings when they were young in both Coventry and Lucknow. There is a growing literature which identifies children's contribution to caring work in families in Britain. Studies have found that children perform a range of jobs caring for their siblings (Gullestad 1988, Kosonen 1996, Morrow 1994, Tatum and Tucker 1998) and for their ill and disabled parents (Segel and Simkins 1993, Aldridge and Becker 1993). In consistent with the findings of existing studies, this study also finds that a majority of children, particularly girls, contributed to caring jobs in ways similar to their parents. On recalling their experience of caring for siblings, Coventry girls reported that they routinely undertook jobs like dressing up, feeding, changing nappies, fetching toddlers to nurseries. Sometimes they took their sick siblings to surgeries to see their family doctor. On asking when they usually looked after their siblings, children reported that they looked after their brothers and sisters during school holidays, after nursery or school and in the evenings. For example, Rita, a 15 year old Coventry girl revealed her experience of caring for her 7 year old sister:

VC: Who used to look after your sister when she was little?

Rita: Me and my mum.

VC: What were you doing for her?

Rita: I was doing almost everything for her.

VC: Why were only you doing everything for her?

Rita: No. .... no I don't mean that only I was doing everything for her. Actually my mum was looking after her in the morning when I was in the school. But when I used to come back my mum had to work in the shop, so I used to do almost everything for Sonia [sister] like my mum. ..... I was feeding her, changing nappies, sterlizing bottles....... and yeah! Sometimes when she used to cry I had to do all efforts to make her happy. Sometimes her cry made me mad, but I had no option but to look after her........ I was busy mostly with her.

VC: Do you still look after her?

Rita: Well, she is seven now so I'm not doing the same jobs for her. But still I do some of her work like ironing her clothes, giving her dinner and fetching her to school.

Pummy (Coventry, 13, F) also reported that her day starts and ends up with caring for her two sisters and a brother aged 8, 6, and two and half years respectively. Their family runs a grocery shop with an off-license which remains open from 8.00 am to 10.00 pm. She described her routine:

Pummy: I get up with the cry of my brother in the morning. He wakes up at about six and starts crying. I've to give him milk to stop him crying. Then I brush and get fresh..... then I make tea and wake my sisters up and ask them to get ready. I prepare something to eat for them and fetch them to school at about half eight. I come back at half three along with them from school.

VC: Then what do you do?

Pummy: I have my meal and serve to my sisters too. ....then I come to shop and stay for some time. In the evening I help my mum in the kitchen and serve food to all.

VC: How much time do you give to your little brother during your holidays?

Pummy: In school holidays I look after him almost all the day to free my mum for doing other important jobs that she can't do in our school days.

Like Rita and Pummy in the above quotes, many other children reported their involvement in caring jobs to a significant amount. It is interesting to note that children in Lucknow are not so involved in caring jobs as those in Coventry. There are two main reasons for the variation in the extent of involvement in caring jobs. Firstly, mothers in Coventry have less or no support from their kin group, which leads them to resort their elder children to provide support and caring. Indian families in Coventry are primarily constituted parents and their children, while in Lucknow families tend to consist of three generations—grandparents, parents and children. All members live together and share the responsibility of caring each other. The second reason is that mothers in Coventry are often more active in their family businesses and which results in relatively less time to undertake caring jobs. Conversely, mothers' involvement in Lucknow in the family shops is more limited. Children's accounts reveal that mothers in these families help their fathers only when there is a shortage of labour. Such as when a father falls ill mother steps in and looks after the counter. Therefore, it suggests that mothers in Lucknow are more integrated into caring jobs thus freeing children from these jobs.

Children's Miscellaneous Activities

Besides the above, the research established that children perform a number of work activities that also require substantial time, energy and commitment. These activities include entertaining family guests and relatives, shopping for the household, receiving telephone calls, posting letters, paying bills, gardening, washing the family car, helping parents in family business and the like. For the purpose of categorising we can call them miscellaneous jobs. Some of these jobs children carry out as part of their daily routine while others are done when required. Although the quantity of these activities varies among children in both Coventry and Lucknow, almost all children studied were required to undertake them.

SECTION II
The Nature of Children's Domestic Activities

After discussing the children's involvement in various types of domestic activities we now move on to consider the nature of their involvement in these activities. The children's accounts in both Coventry and Lucknow reveal four distinctive features: the organised form of activities; those activities involve children on a permanent basis; those activities require children's skill of management; and those activities produce the domestic economy. These features enable us to recognise children's domestic activities as real 'work'.

Children's activities as organised response to domestic labour demand

Children were asked why they do housework. Their accounts reveal that they undertake domestic tasks because they are required to do so. Although sometimes children undertake some jobs because they enjoy them, more often than not they carry out jobs in response to family needs. Here the example of Rita proves instructive. Rita is a 15 year old girl from Coventry whose family runs a busy corner shop and off-license. Her family consists of father who has cardiac trouble, a mother and a younger brother and sister. The mother has to work with the father in the family business all day and has little time for domestic work which has been taken over by Rita. Her explanation for undertaking the responsibility of domestic tasks is:

Rita: You know, my dad is not well and he can't do much work in the shop so my mum has to help him. And she is busy with the shop. Sanj [younger brother] does some of the work but not much. And nobody else is there to do these jobs. So I have to do the jobs.

VC: Does your mum ask you to do the jobs?

Rita: When I was young she used to ask me but now she doesn't need to ask me much. Now I do all the jobs because I understand that I should do. Say ..... we have to eat dinner so we have to cook. And when we eat dinner we have to wash dishes too.

Rita's sense of responsibility for the family enables her to justify her involvement and account is a strong indicator of how she responds to the needs of the family. On realising the labour demand she carries out household tasks in lieu of her mother. Nicky (Coventry, 12, F) said:

Nicky: I do help my mum in the kitchen because nobody else is there to help her.

VC: Does she ask you to help?

Nicky: Sometimes she does but sometimes she doesn't. ..... (pause)...Actually when somebody comes to visit us then she asks me to help in the kitchen.

VC: How do you help her then?

Nicky: I wash dishes. I set the table and serve the food.

VC: Do you do other jobs also?

Nicky: Yes. On weekends I do cleaning and dusting in the morning.

VC: Why doesn't she [mum] do these jobs?

Nicky: She has to do other jobs.

VC: Do you feel that you shouldn't be given these jobs?

Nicky: Yeah! sometimes I do feel but only when I'm tired or I don't get time for my friends. But when I think the importance of these jobs I realise that it is also necessary. Then I think that working is not to be ashamed of. Everyone does jobs in the family so I do.

Nicky's awareness about the need and importance of domestic tasks is a good example of children's response to the demand of domestic labour. She helps her mother in the kitchen not merely because she likes it but also because she feels that her help is required. In her comments she acknowledges that she undertake other housework too because of the need of the family. The similar pattern is also found in Lucknow where children carry out the household tasks by accepting it as the part of their family life. For example, on asking why she involve herself in housework, Radha, (Lucknow, 14, F) explains:

Radha: I do the jobs because I am required to do.

VC: Why do you feel that you are required to do?

Radha: It's necessary to do all this and that's why I do. You don't feel good if your house is dirty. You clean it because you have to clean it. That's why I do sweeping and dusting. It's the same for kitchen work. You don't expect everything from your mummy. You have to share the burden of the housework. That's what I think. If we won't work there will be mess around, so to avoid this I carry out the housework. ....(Laugh) otherwise who likes to do the jobs. If we had options, we would have enjoyed them.

VC: What options you are talking about?

Radha: I mean if you have maid servant for all the time then why do you do housework by your own. You will also prefer everything done by maid and you only enjoy. But I'm afraid, we can't.

Radha's statement also explains that her involvement is also in response to need. There is some evidence of boys also responding to the demands of the family in this way. For example, Ratan (Coventry, 13, M) explains why and how he performs his domestic responsibilities:

Ratan: You know our shop was opened last year only. It

needs a lot of labour to put in. So my mum and dad are busy all the time in it. That's why I take care of myself and my sister.

VC: What do you do for her?

Ratan: In the morning I make sandwiches for her and I fetch her to school. When I come back I look after her studies.

VC: Do you do anything for your mum and dad also?

Ratan: Yes I do. I make tea or coffee when they need it. Sometimes I make sandwiches especially when my mum doesn't get time to come out of the shop.

VC: Do you think that your help in the house jobs is necessary?

Ratan: Yes. I think it is needed. I'm as responsible as my parents really, because it's a family, we all have to do the jobs. I'm doing just for my family not for anybody else. There are always some jobs to be done, that's why we really do it. I care for them and just do it.

Ratan's family consists of his parents and his only sister of aged seven. His experience of household responsibilities clearly reflects the labour demand of the family. As his parents are busy in the shop the responsibility of caring for his younger sister is left to him. He not only cares for his sister but he was also helping his mother in the kitchen work too. Since he is the eldest child in his family, it became his responsibility to support his parents.

The above examples illustrate the domestic activities of children as a purposeful and expedient contribution to the requirement of the family order. They act responsibly for the family by responding to the specific situations as they arise.

Children's domestic activities: A permanent feature of the domestic work order

To explore the frequency of their involvement in domestic activities, children were asked how often they undertake housework. If children were found to be involved only occasionally in domestic tasks, it would be easy to accepted the argument that children's 'help' or 'assistance' to their parents provides an opportunity for them to learn new roles and skills (Thrall 1978, White and Brinkerhoff 1981). However, in this study children revealed that they have undertook the responsibility of housework on a permanent basis and their perennial involvement in the domestic work order suggests a significant contribution. As described in the previous section children both in Coventry and Lucknow were routinely found in whole range of jobs. These children's accounts suggest that domestic activities become a part of their daily life because they are discharging their domestic responsibilities from the very young. For Example, Pummy (Coventry, 13, F) recalls her association with housework responsibilities:

Pummy: I have been responsible for looking after my brother and sisters from the age of six. You know, I'm the eldest child in the family and my brother and a sisters are younger to me. When they were young I had to do most of their jobs (because) my mum and dad were busy with other jobs. Nobody else was there to look after them [younger siblings] ....I used to take of them.

VC: Do you still look after them?

Pummy: Now I don't have to do much caring for them. Only my younger brother, who is nearly three, needs attention. So I look after him only.

VC: Then what is your routine now?

Pummy: Now I spend more time in the kitchen and in cleaning the house.

VC: Do you do kitchen work and cleaning daily?

Pummy: I help in the kitchen everyday, but cleaning and hoovering..... I do it only on weekends.

Like Pummy, there are many other children in Coventry who have reported involvement in housework activities for a considerable time. Children's domestic activities are pivotal in the domestic work order. The domestic work order is constituted in such a way where children's contribution to it becomes essential. This is clear from the statements of Ravi, (Coventry, 12, M):

Ravi: My routine...oh! it's not exciting. I help my mum and dad, go to school and look after the house.

VC: How do you look after the house?

Ravi: I tidy up the rooms, I make tea and coffee...... If they [parents] ask you to do something, I mean,.... it's not as you say no to them. You do whatever is needed, isn't it....(laughs)...

VC: How long have you been doing all this for them?

Ravi: ....well I think I'm helping them since I grew up.

VC: Do you feel that your help makes a big difference in the family?

Ravi: Yeah! I think so, in that sense [working responsibly] I do a lot of jobs, they [parents] can't cope without my help.. it's all the family and everyone's job is important and so my [job].

Almost similar views have been expressed by children in Lucknow about their domestic activities. Puja (Lucknow, 14, F) reveals:

Puja: Well, the jobs [housework] are must. You can't get rid off them, and if you can't then you have to do them daily.... I do jobs not only for me. If it is for me, I would have choice. As, what I do is for the family, I can't leave [the jobs]....

VC: So, do you feel that without your work your family can't run?

Puja: In some way [looking at the demand], yes. If you live in a family you have to do something or other and I think (that) all the [house] jobs are important, whether it's mine or of others'..... a family runs like this..

The above views expressed by children clearly illustrate that children's activities are permanent. The contexts of their activities explain their involvement in household activities not only in response to the demand for labour but also as a permanent arrangement. Wherever they are found to be contributing this is usually inevitable. They have taken up the responsibility of housework not because they wish to take it, but because it is mandatory. The extent of involvement of children in domestic activities may differ between Coventry and Lucknow, but the frequency of their recurrence remains the same. The degree of labour demand for children's domestic activities may differ in Coventry and Lucknow but their involvement is indisputable. This is the point of resemblance which gives force to the claim that children's activities are inevitable and a permanent response to the labour demand. Children's positive response to this demand maintains the domestic work order of which both parents and children are a part.

The management of time and ideas in children's domestic activities

To explore the nature of children's domestic activities further, questions were asked about the children's control over domestic activities. Their experiences reveal some intriguing facts about their management skills. Although they expressed their indispensability in the domestic work order, their experiences inform us how they manage the time and ideas. They do not always succumb to all situations. They do not undertake all the jobs they are asked to, but sometimes manipulate the situation to perform these jobs in the way that they want to. This is evident in Pummy's case where she has responsibility of caring for her younger brother.

Pummy: He [younger brother] is very demanding. I know what to be given to make him happy. Sometimes he really makes me mad but I know how to deal with. ...

VC: Can you describe your experiences?

Pummy: ....(thinking) ...Oh! Yeah. If we leave him alone [younger brother] he makes a mess and we have to clean it up,..... it's just the way he mess that gets me down. You know what I do when I'm busy with other things.... I just switch on the cartoon network on telly to keep him busy. That's what I do...........You know he's mad after *'flinstones'* and *'scooby doo'*. I've got some videos of them. Look when I've my things to do and to look after him too then I put on videos. He gets busy with them and let me do my work...otherwise it's hard to work with him really.

Pummy's idea of how to look after her brother while working reflects certain management skills and like some of the other children, she translates her ideas into practice. Similarly, Rita's (Coventry, 15, F) example of carrying out the kitchen work exemplifies the management of time. She describes:

Rita: If I've to go out with my friends I finish the cooking early.

VC: Are you free to do cook whenever you want?

Rita: Yes. I'm. It's all up to me.... Sometimes I make *sabzi* [vegetable curry] in the evening and I make *rotti* [chapatti] at the dinner time when everybody is on the table. But that's not fixed. I do it as my convenience. Like if I have to do something important or I've to watch telly I finish the cooking before or leave it for later on. .... I prefer to wash dishes in the night but if it's too late or I'm tired I leave it for the next morning.

Rita's description informs us that although she has to work in the kitchen daily she has control over the management of time and the menu. Like caring and kitchen work children are also found to use their skills in house-maintenance work. For example Rahul (Lucknow, 14, M) describes:

Rahul: In the last month we had white wash in our house. I did whatever I could.

VC: What did you do?

Rahul: I re-arranged my bed room and the lounge.

VC: Did anybody tell you how to do it?

Rahul: No. My parents only ask me to do but the way I wanted to do, I did. Like I was planning to change the set up of the lounge for long and I changed it then.

VC: Are you always free to do the jobs as you want them to?

Rahul: Most of the time I'm free. Like my papa asked me to pay the electricity bill but it is up to me when I'll pay it. I'm going to pay it tomorrow because today I'm going somewhere else.So this is the way I do the house jobs.

Rahul's use of his management skills is apparent in his description of household activities. The above illustrations demonstrate how children use their skills of management of time and ideas in undertaking their domestic activities. The important point to noted here is that children in Coventry and Lucknow are equally good in using their capabilities in the management of domestic activities. The study further finds some interesting examples of where children demonstrated that they not only use their skills in doing household jobs but also enter into a negotiation process to achieve their motives.

Children's domestic activities and the domestic economy

The domestic activities of children not only involve management skills, but also provide a source of conversion of family's resources too. Children's participation in domestic activities provides an opportunity for the family to substantiate its economy. There is some evidence from Coventry where children reported that in the last few of years their family businesses had expanded and their parents, particularly mothers, involvement in the family shop became more intense. In other situations children reported that they have undertaken household responsibilities in lieu of their mothers from the last few years. Looking at these facts, it can be seen that children's household responsibilities have direct link with their mothers' increased contribution to the family business. This is evident in Rajni's (Coventry, 10, F) case who says

Rajni: My mum and dad do most of the work in the shop.

VC: Could you please tell me what they do in shop?

Rajni: They do all the jobs.....they serve the counter, bring the stuff from the warehouse. They put all the goods in the proper place.

VC: How is your business?

Rajni: It's good. We didn't have off license until last Christmas. In the last Christmas we have got off-license to sell spirits. Now our shop is busy. Our shop is extended now and we started selling the range of Asian food .... it's like mini-super market.

VC: Then there must be more demand of work in it.

Rajni: Yes. There is. But now my mum helps my dad in it..... Sometimes my brother does some of the jobs. Even I sometimes help them. So it's ok.

VC: If your mum works in the shop then how does she manage to do housework?

Rajni: Now I handle some of the housework...Like I wash dishes, I make tea and sandwiches and set lay the table and yeah! .....I do all the work in my room too.

VC: How long you have been doing these jobs?

Rajni: Since I was eight.

In Rajni's statements, it can be seen that as she took on some of her mother's responsibility of housework, her mother was freed for domestic work. Because of her mother's greater availability of time and labour the shop expanded and the family enjoyed greater economic returns. Like Rajni, Pummy also recalled looking after her brother instead of sending him to a child minder. Her decision to look after him by herself was to some extent motivated by the anticipated savings to the family.

Like Rajni and Pummy there were also other children in Coventry whose domestic activities did not expose the full implications of their undertaking of household responsibilities. Their explanations regarding the household responsibilities show how they release other family members primarily their mothers to give more time to family business. In Lucknow, as noted earlier, the social context is different from that of Coventry. Due to this, mothers usually do not spend much time in shops in comparison to housework. However, the demand of domestic work is heavier so that many resort to in listing the help of either by paid maid-servants or their own children. Certainly the children from Lucknow helped their families in this way as in the case of Smiriti's (Lucknow, 15, F) example:

Smiriti: Earlier a maid was doing dishwashing. But for the last six months I have been doing it in the evening?

VC: Why have you started doing it?

Smiriti: Because my mummy says that I am grown up and I should do it.

VC: Ok. Your are grown up, but if you can afford to have a maid then why do you take up these jobs?

Smiriti: Well, I have taken this job because my mummy

explained me that if we do by our own we can save some money, which she says that we can spend on us...and to some extent I do agree with her.

Smiriti's involvement in extra kitchen work explains that it is a deliberate attempt to save family money. Through saving the expenditure incurred in hiring a maid, she decided to contribute to the domestic economy. The illustrations cited above show that the outcome of these activities is accountable in economic terms. This satisfies the definition of work, one of whose central ingredients is that its output should be economically meaningful. The intrinsic worth of unremunerative activities is utilized by parents and this transfer of transaction does not take away or reduce the economic value of children's activities.

There has been no evidence in our case to show that children either in Coventry or Lucknow have ever been paid for domestic work, a finding in-line with those of Brannen's (1995) study. However, she does cite the statement of a British father who paid his three daughters, admitting that they were 'paid a wage like hired cleaners' (1995:329). In Coventry the children were indirectly responsible for augmenting family income. If Indian children never received payment for housework this can straight-away be explained by strong cultural traditions in which relations and services over-ride the economic considerations. Whether the evidence is direct or indirect, children's activities in such circumstances provide proof of their contribution to the domestic economy.

SECTION III

Children's Domestic Activities: A vital Contribution to Domestic Work

One of the basic premises of study reported here is that children's contribution to domestic work has until recently been neglected due to a lack of empirical evidence. The major reason for this neglect is the limited scope of definition of work.

Whether children's domestic activities can amount to work can be established only on the resemblance of outstanding features of the activities to the ingredients of work. To examine this, the extent and nature of children's domestic activities are explored by taking evidence from Coventry and Lucknow. The children in the study reported here provide strong evidence of substantial involvement in domestic work. The amount of their domestic activities and its nature suggests their contribution is not less important, if not equal than that of their parents in the division of domestic labour.

Morrow (1996) has remarked that the notion of work changes from person to person but this need to be questioned. For example, what is work for a mother when she dresses her children does not remain so when children dress themselves. I have started with a further examination of this point empirically. The self-provisioning activities display that the work of child-care is a case of direct transfer from mother to children. The transfer of work from mother to child is an interesting transaction for analysis. Outwardly there are three distinct stages which start with 'help' then pass on to 'sharing' and ultimately culminate in the replacement of adults' work. Some research has taken note of the fact that mothers seek children's help but the implication of this request for help has not been probed. I have found in this study that mothers do not ask for help until they are sure that the children are able to give it. Not only mothers but even children do not come forward for help until they feel their work is of desirable standard. The transaction even at the initial stage is a two way affair. It relies upon acceptance of children's capacity in the context. What is called sharing is a step further than help because it amounts to independently taking over part of, or partial replacement of the work of the adult. The complete transfer of mother's work, for example child caring and kitchen related work, is solid proof of total conviction of the capacity of the transferee that is children. The three stages from help to replacement therefore display an increasing degree of realization in the capacity of children to work in the family. This picture contradicts the earlier idea of children's incompetence as workers.

It is interesting to note here that the children's self-provisioning activities are not a case of the simple transfer of work as it demands a continuation of the standard. When mothers find children's work falling below the standard they readily step in and make up the deficiency. The retention of the same quality of work by children is an indication of their exertion both at the mental and physical level which constitutes an important ingredient of work. This analysis clearly shows that children's activities of these kinds are fully on a par with mother's child care work and that they constitute a solid contribution to the domestic work order.

As regards children's involvement in housework Gill (1998) has argued that parents adopt different strategies like appreciation, reward and punishment in assigning work. The evidences in this study demonstrate a different strategy based on children's ability to work. The family set-up is found to have a hierarchy and an organised domestic work order consisting of simple and complex activities forming part of a set pattern. Children's activities are performed under these specific well laid out conditions. The developmental view has seen children's performance of household work as their 'styles of learning' which are integral to 'pattern of socialization' (Goodnow, 1988). The findings in this study contradict this view and prove that these activities are not mere 'learning' but are an organised response to specific demands of the domestic work order of the family. These activities are not only useful for the doer but equally useful for other members of the family. These activities are found to be affecting mothers in particular. Mother's participation in family businesses is affected by children's undertaking of self provisioning and household responsibilities. These features of activities satisfy the ingredient of work (in the extended definition).

It has been found in this study that children's routine domestic activities are a permanent feature of the domestic work order. These activities involve the achieved and inherent skills of children. When mother takes care of little children the skill is presumed and when this task is transferred to young children for their siblings the same presumption of skill is continued. This fact patently contradicts the view that children's domestic activities are only learning because learning is a period of acquiring skills. The adherence to time adds to the importance of these activities. The willing responsiveness of children covers both permanent and temporary activities. It has also been noted that the nature of temporary activity does not mean that it is in any way less demanding in respect of skill. The gravity of the family demand in both is matched by the responsiveness of the child who is expected to rise up to the occasion. The general ethos of work found in the families is redolent of the mandatory atmosphere of these activities. In the pattern of distribution of work every member has to work strictly according to the set pattern. Just like adults, children pull their full weight wherever they have to perform an activity. Brannen (1995) has found that children have a better scope for voluntary participation in tasks of family care than in self-care work. This study also finds that sometimes children undertake unassigned housework too, which suggests that there is a scope for children to participate voluntarily in household jobs.

Morrow (1996) has called for an analysis of children's economic activities within the home in order to reconsider the domestic division of labour. In this study children's domestic activities have been discussed to find out how, if at all, they are related to the domestic economy. It has been found that not only do children offer help or share in domestic activities but that they also replace adults completely, so enabling the adults (mothers) to work in their family business which in turn results in higher economic returns. The intrinsic value of children adopting activities from their mothers is clearly cashed in by the spared member of the family. Their contribution to the reproduction of the domestic economy therefore stands out and cannot be played down by anyone. It is always forthcoming. This feature of children's activities is in conformity with the ingredient of work which is understood to have a return in terms of economic value. The question whether it is direct or indirect is immaterial.

6

THE MEANING AND SIGNIFICANCE OF CHILDREN'S DOMESTIC WORK

It has been argued in the previous chapter that children's domestic activities need serious consideration as work, especially given that they are not only significantly involved in them, but their activities have social and economical influence on the family. Children have been found to contribute to domestic work and are not simply objects who create work for others or who themselves are products of adults' reproductive domestic labour. One view is that children's work is a consequence of parents' strategies to involve them (Gill 1998) and the other view is that it is an instrument of their development (White and Brinkerhoff 1981). Both the views are an outside imposition on the status of children's work. The argument developed in this study is, however, different. It is argued that children are not just a cog in the machine, but when placed in the family their work is socially meaningful in its own terms. It seems, therefore, vital that children's experiences and reactions to their domestic work be considered seriously. The key questions of this chapter, therefore, are: how children experience their work and what meaning do they assign to it?; and how is their work significant for themselves as well as for the whole family? On ground of children's agency, it will be explored whether children turn out to be social actors who contribute to the construction of their childhood as well as to the maintenance of the family through their involvement in domestic work.

It is children's experience of various routine household activities which justify them as their contribution to domestic work. Children articulate social meanings to their activities. The experience children have of various types of domestic work is a potent factor in influencing them while attributing a meaning it has for them. Children's experience of activities involves their contextual complexities and their own predilections. All of these protean but potential factors play a paramount role in the transaction which forms an area of great interest during examination. The meanings of domestic work for children include the conditions which prompt them to work and the reasons for their justification. In this light, the first section of this chapter addresses specifically the desirability and utility of children's work, the qualitative features of children's work are on the same lines as that of adults and children's concern for the family as a source of their involvement. The meanings derived from cultural forces are subsequently addressed in order to get a complete picture of the meanings of children's domestic work.

The overarching question to be answered in the second section is what significance do the meanings, which children ascribed to their domestic work, have and for whom? Two directions of inquiry are taken up — domestic work as an index of their responsibility and as a medium of their autonomy. In the last section I discuss how far children's domestic work is found to affect their childhood and the social order of the family. The main argument of this chapter is that domestic work paves the way for responsibility and autonomy which again help them to realsie their distinct position in the family. Domestic work helps to redefine their childhood in a different way to whatever has been said about them so far. The domestic work is also seen as an instrument of children for structuring and re-structuring family life.

The Meanings of Domestic Work from Children's Perspective

Our discussion in the previous chapter clearly establishes the fact that children's domestic activities are an organised response to the demand for labour. It is also illustrated that they are aware of their work-roles. The moment when they begin to give importance to their activities particularly for the family, the activities become socially meaningful. Their involvement in various stages of the domestic work order makes them important members of the family. Their varied experience in these stages provides a base for constructing the meanings of various types of work. The way they construct these meanings depends on how they respond to the various work situations that arise. The factors that influence them are both internal and external. The primary factor is internal as their experience and reactions are *ab initio* subjective. The other factor which is external includes several causal conditions which either prompt or impede the reactions. These could be enumerated, in short, as the family's social order, its organised work pattern, and the child's subordinate position in the hierarchical order of the family.

The desirability of children's work

Consistent with Seymour's (1988) findings, children in both Coventry and Lucknow reported that they undertake different types of jobs as responsible members of cooperative and interdependent households. Their work is a desirable act for the maintenance of the family. This is tangibly explained by Roop (Coventry, 15, F) in her following conversation:

Roop: We are working at home because everybody is working at home and if we don't work then who will do it? This is our house and we have to do the jobs. I don't mind in doing housework...... I am the eldest in the family and if I help my parents with the housework then my sister will follow me. And afterall we are working for ourselves so, nothing wrong in it......

VC: So, do you think that you are working at home because everybody is doing so?

Roop: Yes, of course. In our Asian society we all are working at home and we share our responsibility of house work. House work is not only a parents duty. Like making our beds and washing and ironing our clothes is our responsibility. Who else will do housework if we don't? Nobody. So, we have to do it all. Like cooking.... We have to eat our meals so we have to cook and that's why we cook.

Roop's statement displays the two very important factors in children's assessments of housework: desirability and utility. She recognises her contribution to housework as both necessary and helpful for the whole family. For instance, she maintains that both cooking and ironing are reproductive work and are obvious. She recognises that home is a place where all have to work since every family members' work is necessary for the reproduction of the family. This is also strengthened by the nature of its continuity. If she takes over part of her parents' housework her sister will also get involved. Sanjay (Lucknow, 15, M) comments on his contribution:

Sanjay: I like shopping and that is why I always go to market to buy vegetables and other daily items for our home.

VC: Do you always do the shopping?

Sanjay: Yes. Most of the time I do it.

VC: When do you do it?

*Sanjay:*Whenever anything is required in the kitchen or at home, then my mummy asks me to go to the shop and buy that. Sometimes when any guests come then my mummy also asks me to buy some refreshments or savouries from the nearby shops.

VC: How long have you been doing this type of shopping?

Sanjay: I think when I was nine or ten I started going to the shop.

VC: Do you feel that this work is necessary for the family?

Sanjay: Yes. The family cannot run without shopping.

VC: But why do you do it?

Sanjay: My dad is busy in the shop and my mummy looks

after the housework so I have to do it.

Sanjay maintains that for the maintenance of the family shopping cannot be avoided and his family needs him to do shopping. It seems that he undertakes mainly those jobs for the family that are different to that of Roop above, although both the children undertake these jobs in similar ways. The desirability of their work is a common experience of both the children. Similarly, children who are working as 'carers' for their siblings also emphasise the usefulness of caring jobs for the smooth functioning of the family. Rita (Coventry, 15, F) who reported her caring jobs gave the reason for them:

Rita: I shared my mum's responsibility to look after my sister because there was no other option..... We had to share it, ..when (my) mum had to work in the shop then I used to do housework and look after Sonia [younger sister]. .... I remember those days when I was going to our friends house I had to take my sister with me, but she [friend] never brought her brother who was also little like Sonia to our house. Actually, her grandmother used to look after her brother. But in our family we had no support. ...It was all embracing for me to take Sonia everywhere, I had to.

The above three quotes illustrate the conditions in which these children contribute to domestic work. Roop's house-maintenance activities, Sanjay's participation in outdoor jobs and Rita's caring for her younger sister all demonstrate a common feature. All these children undertake their respective routine domestic responsibilities because they themselves feel that their involvement is/was necessary for the maintenance of the family. Apart from routine housework children undertake occasional work too, particularly in contingent situations. This occasional work should not, however, be deemed unimportant or negligible because of its periodic existence. It is, at least, as significant as routine work because it requires considerable understanding from children in response to complex situations. Children's accounts show that are able to assess the full implications of the meanings which they themselves assign to the occasional work in the contingent/critical situations. This is evident in Kiran's (Coventry, 14, F) experiences. She has a small family consisting of a younger brother and a sister. She explained that six months back her father was hospitalised for two weeks on account of a kidney disorder. Her mother had therefore to look after her husband and also the family business. Kiran, as a result, had to do all the housework and even missed school to meet the crisis. She explains:

*Kiran:*If I had been going to school those days then my Mum would have looked after my brother and sister and the house. And in that case she would have to close the shop and that was not possible because it is our only source of income. And if our income stops then you can't pay bills.

VC: So, do you think that there was no option?

Kiran: Yes. Of course. I am the eldest child in the family. I had to run the house and help my mum in the situation. It was hard time for all of us and there was no way out.

In almost similar circumstances Renu (Lucknow, 15, F) whose father had gone blind a few years back explained that she worked at home not only because she wanted to but because she recognised its need. She says:

*Renu:*I work for the family. I am related to my family and since my family needs [work to be done], so I do it. If I work at home than it doesn't mean that I like the work. I work because I feel that my work is necessary for the family.

VC: Don't you feel that you take care of your father and your younger brother because you like them?

Renu: Yes I like them but that's not all. I work for them not just because I like them. It's work which has to be done. Without that [housework] we all suffer, so we do it.

VC: Do you mean that your contribution is the most needed and valuable work in the family?

Renu: Yes. Of course, I do.

Both situations illustrate the awareness of these girls of their importance to the family during period of crisis. Their replies illustrate their awareness of the necessity and utility of their work. For them housework is obligatory, which must be done whether they like it or not. Besides the crisis situations children were found to be heavily involved in house-maintenance work in certain occasions. The additional work during festivals represents an additional burden on every member in the Indian family, including children. They take up the jobs by recognising their need for the family. For instance, Ravi (Coventry, 12, M) says:

Ravi: I like helping my dad decorating the house.

VC: How often do you do it?

Ravi: Not very often. Like last Christmas we changed the wall paper of this room. Before that this showcase was in that corner but we have changed its position and kept it here. I like organising the room.

VC: Why did you do it?

Ravi: If I did not do it then some outsider would have come to help my mum and dad. ......I also like decorating so I could save unnecessary expenses.

Similarly Rahul (Lucknow, 14, M) reports his increased house maintenance work during festival days:

VC: When do you do more house work?

Rahul: Especially during festival days I have to do a lot of work.

VC: What do you do then?

Rahul: As you know before *Diwali* we have to whitewash and paint our house and clean it up. So I do it along with my parents and hired labour. I re-organise my whole house.

VC: What are the other festivals when you have to do this much work?

Rahul: On *Holi* as well. But on *Holi* we don't have white wash in the house so we simply clean our house as many relatives and friends used to come to our house to greet us.

In both Coventry and Lucknow annual festivals require extra work for house-maintenance in the shape of a face-lift. This is a demand of the family to which children react positively. The palpable desirability and the definite utility of this added work are clear from their views. The clarity with which all the above quoted children recognise the importance of their work not only underlines their awareness of themselves and their work as crucial to the maintenance of the family, but also highlights their ability as active and responsive actors. Their contextualisation of the work, which they undertake in crisis situations or during festivals, is a strong example of how children give the social meanings to their work. It is also important to note that children's contextualisation of their work with the needs of their families is common in Coventry and Lucknow. This suggests that desirability of children's work and children's subsequent response to those needs do not differ with the different locations of these Indian families.

Children's attempt to rationalise their work

From an outside view it is regarded that children's domestic work resemble to adults work as they copy adults. However, this study finds that children as rational people have an understanding of their contribution to the maintenance of the family. They also have a sense of the importance of their contributions *vis-à-vis* their parents. This is evident in Dinky's (Coventry, 14, F) contribution to her family. She recalled an incident when her father visited her grandfather in India for five weeks during the previous year. Her mother had to look after the family business in her father's absence and she had to look after all the domestic responsibilities, which meant she had to miss her studies for few days. She not only managed the housework but also contributed to the family business with the help of her mother. When asked how she felt about her housework, Dinky said:

Dinky: I worked hard at that time. It was a very busy time for all of us. My mum was working at the shop and I was looking after the house which was quite heavy. I was making breakfast, preparing meals, washing dishes and hoovering. And yeah! I was cleaning the house.

VC: But people say that children can't work like parents. What do you think about it?

Dinky: No. If they say so, they are wrong. I don't agree with this view. It is wrong to underestimate us.....See I did all the work which my mum normally did. Even now I am working as much as my parents. I am sure that my work is like their work.

VC: How do your parents look at your contributions?

Dinky: My mum and dad both appreciate it.

VC: How?

Dinky: They are happy to see me do all the work. Sometimes they praise me.

It may be noted that it is not only Dinky who thinks that her work is as good as her parents, they also acknowledge this to be so. Their positive reaction adds to the significance of the meaning Dinky attaches to her work. Dinky's statement also underlines that the importance attached to their work is not only periodic but a routine feature of family life. The most important aspect in Dinky's statement is that she rationalises her contribution with her parent's contribution. Similar views of rationalisation of their work are evident in Rita (Coventry, 15, F) statements:

VC: Don't you think that it's easy for your mum to cook food ?

Rita: No no.. it's not so. She takes the same time what I take.

VC: May be she is cooking meals for ages, so she cooks better than you.

Rita: No I don't agree with you. I believe that I do the same work that my mum does and we both have to spend the same energy and time in cooking food.

VC: Except cooking what are the other works that you and your mum both do?

Rita: We wash dishes, tidy up the rooms, clean and hoover and dusting.

VC: Does your mum do any of this work quicker than you?

Rita: No I don't think so. I am as quick as my mum ...... Since I have been doing all this for the last couple of years it has come second nature and now I can do these more quickly and expertly.

Both, the way these children argue the qualitative

importance of their work and the evidence about the quantity of their work in their statements, suggest that whatever their position in the power relationship with the parents the value of their work is seen to be similar to their parent's work. Lucknow children reported the similar views. For example, Sehar (Lucknow, 13, F) believes that her work is no less important than that of her mother.

VC: Do you think that you can do all the work that your parents usually do at home?

Saher: Yes. Why not? I can do everything. Some of them I do daily.

VC: Have you ever felt that your work is in any way inferior to your parents?

Saher: No. no no ....Never. Yes sometimes my mummy cooks food better than me but it doesn't mean that what I cook is inferior to my mummy's. I do cleaning and sometimes my mummy does. Both are equally good so in what respect is my work less than my mummy [work].

VC: Has nobody ever said that your work is not up to the mark?

Saher: It may not be up to the mark sometimes, but only when I am not in a mood for some reason. But normally it is not so. It does not mean that my work is not as valuable as that of my parents. Basically we both work for the each other, so It [my work] has same value what their's [parents] work has.

Neither the child is a scaled-down version of the adult nor is his /her work a scaled-down version of the adult's work, as is often argued. The evidence here shows that the children's work appears to be of equal value as that of their parents. Those exceptional circumstances in which it has been found to be below par are quite usual in the ordinary run of the domestic work. It only goes to strengthen the veracity of children's statements in general.

Children's concern of social relationships and their work

In recounting their experience of domestic work children

reveal several aspects of their capacities and competencies. An interesting and so far undisclosed aspect is seen in Pummy's case in Coventry which reveals her acute sensibility and daring in the event of crisis or emergency. Pummy's parents strictly follow the Indian tradition of taking their children with them in social gatherings such as marriages and birthday parties. Child care is, therefore, not a normal issue except in the case of her parents' illness when Pummy has to manage it. Explaining how Pummy (Coventry, 13, F) does it she says:

Pummy: (after thinking) ... Oh. Yeah! I can tell you an event. Last year my sister had chicken pox and didn't go to school for about fifteen days. On those days I was taking care of my younger brother as he was too little. My sister wasn't allowed to go around and she was at home.

VC: Why did she have to stay at home?

Pummy: Since she had chicken pox she could not go to school or out of the house as it was infectious.

VC: How did you manage it then?

Pummy: I had looked after her and others too. That was terribly difficult for me. I didn't go to my school for a week. I was looking after the kitchen and both (my) sister and brother.

VC: Ok. Did you have no fear of infection?

Pummy: I didn't care since I had to....... I cared for her because I love her.

VC: Ok. Don't you feel over burdened at such a time?

Pummy: Yes. I do. Sometime when I missed my school...... But not always.

VC: What are the other occasions when you missed your school?

Pummy: I had to miss my school only when I felt that I had to take care of the sick and help my parents. For example my dad fell ill, my mother had to take over extra work in the shop and I had to do cooking and cleaning.

Pummy's description brings out the limits of her concern for the family as well as the degree of her contribution to meet the crisis. Facing illness involves a premium on her duty to care followed by her love for her sister and mother. This order of expression is indicative of almost an adult-like sensibility and devotion. Missing school for caring purposes buttresses the argument. The following illustration gives another picture of children's serious concern for the maintenance of social relationship, particularly in caring work. Jyoti (Lucknow, 10, F) expresses:

Jyoti: I like my *dadi* [Grandmother] and *baba* [Grandfather] too much but I didn't like their work.

VC: What work?

Jyoti: Giving medicine, taking them to the toilet when they are ill, taking them out for a walk. I liked serving tea or whatever. I liked talking with them and I was talking too much. But I don't like to take them for an evening walk.

VC: Why didn't you like his evening walk?

Jyoti: Because that was my play time and he wanted to go out and walk around.

VC: How often were you taking him out for a walk?

Jyoti: Sometime I was taking him out or sometimes my sister took him out.

VC: Did you enjoy your grandparents' stay with you?

Jyoti: Yes, we enjoyed it.

VC: But you have said that you didn't like his evening walk.

Jyoti: ......Yeah! I didn't like his walk but I liked them very much. That's why I took him for a walk.

The concern that Jyoti expresses for her grandparents has many interesting strands. She is prepared to take care of them, even escorting them to the toilet. This manifests a more serious concern than serving tea. However, her outspokenness makes her concede that she did not like taking her grandfather out for a walk in the evening because of its conflict with her play time. What deserves credit in this situation is that though she is hardly 10 she can overcome her desire to play when the social relationship in the family requires her services for grandfather.

Children's concern for social relationship in the family in both Coventry and Lucknow gets reflected in their contributions to domestic work. This can be gathered from their alacrity to act, degree of exertion and perseverance in performance despite handicaps — all of which show their work almost as significant as that of adults though it may not sound so in all terms. Despite the difference in cultural conditions in Coventry and Lucknow, there is little difference in children's reactions and meanings which they assign to working as carers.

The cultural meanings of domestic work

Children are found to articulate the meanings of their work in cultural terms too. The specific cultural values of these Indian families have direct bearings on children's understanding of their domestic work responsibilities. Children maintain their family norms through domestic work. The cultural traditions of India permeate the Indian families so deeply that it sets the norms for the domestic work in a number of different situations. For example, the tradition of hospitality is derived from the Indian culture and its classical literature which speaks not only of great respect for mother and father (in the saying *'matra devo bhav'* and *'pitra devo bhav'*) but also of treating guests like Gods (*'atithi devo bhav'*). The hospitality, which includes greeting, seating and serving guests, reflects the family's prestige and status. As Seymore (1988) observed, Indian children normally carry out these tasks with full sense of responsibility to maintain their family's socio-cultural prestige.

The feature of extended family among Indians is attributable to this phenomenon. The close-knit relationship which extends beyond a family is both the cause and effect of the continuance of this feature of these families. Just as Indian families do not allow their children to let the side down, and see to it that they keep up their prestige in the community, so they also ensure a careful compliance with a family's traditional values and norms. How children react and give meaning to this special type of work emerged as an interesting dimension to the research.

Smiriti (Lucknow, 15, F) provides an illustration:

Smiriti:......Once I was listening to music in my room when I heard my mummy. She was calling me to come downstairs. When I asked why I had to come down she said, "Look your

Buaji [father's sister] has come". Then I went down and saw my *Buaji* in the sitting room. I sat with her for some time. Then my mummy asked me to bring something for her to drink. I called her in and then asked "why don't you?" Then she said "I am with Buaji". Then I went to the kitchen and served her tea. After some time she left and then I came back to my room........... I didn't like being disturbed but I had to.

VC: But why?

Smiriti: Because if I wouldn't have come down and made tea for her then it would have sullied my mummy's name.

VC: How?

Smiriti: They might think that my parents have not taught me good manners. That's why I have to do this work.

VC: But your maid servant can serve tea or whatever? Why had you to serve?

Smiriti: No, in my family if close relatives come then we serve food or tea to them. Maid servants can help us in making tea alright, but we are supposed to serve it ourselves. It doesn't look nice that we ask our servants to serve drinks to our guests especially relatives.

*VC:*So what do you feel about this?

Smiriti:..... (smiles)... Oh! I don't want to be disturbed but in these circumstances what can we do except to do it? We can't escape it. We have to do this work. It doesn't matter whether we like it or not.

This illustration shows a degree of ambivalence. Smiriti understands the gravity of this special domestic work as is clear from her knowledge of family traditions. Failure to meet the general expectation of the family in cultural terms and not doing a task like this can cast a slur upon the family. The meaning which she ascribes to this specific work includes an understanding of its delicacy as well as its utility for herself as much as for the family. Her work meets two simultaneous demands: the first is the maintenance of the household and the second is the maintenance of cultural traditions.

What obtains in Coventry families can be gathered from the version of Rita (Coventry, 15, F) which displays that though she herself likes English food she has to learn how to prepare Indian food because of the cultural requirements that demand an Indian girl to conduct herself in appropriate ways:

Rita: I cook all Indian and English food. My mum and dad prefer to take Indian food but we prefer English.

VC: What do you cook for your Indian meal?

Rita: Curry, rice, chapati and all that.

VC: Why do you cook Indian food when you prefer English?

Rita: I cook Indian food because everyone else likes it. My mum tells me that I will be required to cook Indian food when I go to my in-laws? That's why I give more time to it.

VC: How do you take it?

Rita: I don't mind cooking Indian food, but I don't agree with my mum. I like to cook Indian dishes because most of my family take it at least once a day..... To some extent our food is our identity. You know many white people like Indian food. They come to our shop or to Indian restaurants just because of Indian dishes. I think every Indian should know how to cook Indian food. This will definitely bringa distinct identity to our families.

VC: How do you feel that it will bring a distinct identity to you or your family?

Rita: Because we are Indians and most of the Indian people in Britain still prefer taking Indian food. And we eat Indian dishes we keep ourselves as Indians.

VC: How long have you been cooking Indian food?

Rita: Since I was 11 or 12.

Rita's reaction to her mother's expectations regarding the cooking of Indian dishes explicitly tells us why she cooks Indian dishes. The general assumption is that Indian children cook Indian dishes because their parents want them to grow up as Indians, and while that is true in Rita's parents case too her comments present a different picture. Her explanation for cooking Indian meals is not a role-rehearsal or socialization into cultural traditions. It is also about keeping the family's cultural values intact.

Apart from some similarities among children in Coventry and Lucknow, the difference in exercising the agency to gain the independence between Coventry and Lucknow children has been noted. The children of Coventry are able to exercise more independence than those at Lucknow. Probably this is on account of the interaction with British social conditions through education and life-style. This is evident from the conversation Gur (Coventry,14, F):

Gur: I receive family guests when my parents are at home. I also offer them a seat, tea and snacks.

VC: What happens when your parents are not at home?

Gur: Normally I don't want to entertain guests of my parents in their absence.

VC: Don't they ask you to entertain them when they are not at home?

Gur: Yes. They did say so. Earlier I was taking care of guests but now I don't. I feel bored. They are not of my age. I have already told my mum that I won't sit with them whom I don't like.

VC: What have your parents said then to you?

Gur: She felt bad but she doesn't force me.

Rita's and Gur's comments show that the influence of Indian cultural tradition in these Coventry children has not entirely faded out. There is a degree of resistance and independence between the two sets of children. Those in Lucknow quietly give in to the traditional norms while this is not so with the children in Coventry.

Children's view of the extra amount of domestic work in terms of entertaining guests, as noted above, is coloured by its cultural meaning. Children tailor their domestic work to suit this meaning. They institutionalise the cultural values through this work.

The Significance of Children's Domestic Work

As socially active people, children rationalise about what they do and also about what others in the family do. It is fairly clear by now that their domestic work is not a leisure time activity, but it is an organised response to the labour demand of the family. Thus, their understanding about the needs of the family provides a basis for their contribution. They try to see sense in everything around them and do not go on household errands for fun. They do most of the work at home either because they feel it is necessary and useful or else because they are asked to do it. Having established these points, I intend to examine the implications of their work for themselves in the following paragraphs. This attempt will highlight the significance of children's domestic work.

Children's domestic work as an index of responsibility

If we were to sketch out how domestic work is assigned, it would be apparent that it is broadly divisible into the categories of pre-assigned, assigned, and unassigned work. The pre-assigned work (which we have earlier noted as routine work) is an acknowledgment of the child's competency and the unassigned is a challenge to both their sense of responsibility and competence. Help in the kitchen belongs to the first category and the entertainment of expected guests in the presence of parents falls under the second. However, if guests drop in without notice in the absence of parents the case would be an example of unassigned work. Arrival of guests in the presence of parents is comparatively an easier situation because parents are available to provide instructions and guidance. In the latter case, however, the challenge to their sense of responsibility and competence is more demanding. The element of responsibility is to be found inherent in all conditions of domestic work starting from the pre-assigned to the unassigned in growing degrees. Children in both Coventry and Lucknow are found expressing their responsibile behaviour in all such situations. They have fully met the challenge to their developing sense of actorship through their sense of responsibility.

Nicky, a Coventry girl of 12, has two brothers, one younger and the other older than her. Because of some family problems her parents moved from Birmingham to Coventry about a year before our conversation. According to Nicky they are working hard to establish the new business and Nicky frees her mother from caring for her four year old brother so that she can concentrate on the shop. During the conversation Nicky reported that she undertakes the responsibility of looking after her brother, which includes partly assigned and partly unassigned work. She reported an incident of her unassigned work:

Nicky: Yesterday Avi fell down when he was playing. He hit himself and his knee was cut. There was blood coming. I took him inside and wiped the knee with the tissue. When it was dry I put some cream and a plaster on it. When my mum came back than I told her about the accident.

VC: What did she say?

Nicky: She said "It's all right".

VC: Why did you do it?

Nicky: Nobody was there and I was the eldest there. He was crying very badly and I couldn't wait for my mum. That's why.

Leena (Coventry, 13, F) discloses the unassigned jobs which she undertook:

Leena: Last week my dad and mum had gone to the warehouse and me and my brother were at the shop. Then I saw my *masi* [mother's sister] with her cousins who came from Nottingham to visit us. I took them inside and offered drinks. My brother looked after the shop and I was sitting with them. After a while they left.

VC: Then what happened?

Leena: When my parents came back I told them who had come and what I did. They said O.K.

VC: Do you always entertain guests?

Leena: Yes. I normally entertain them but if there is nobody at home then I feel I must do it. .....Normally, if any relative comes to our house then we are supposed to offer tea or drinks and sit with them.

In both Nicky's and Leena's description the parents were

absent and the children's competency and potential for responsibility were called into play. Both instances show that children's sense of responsibility appears toequal to any adult members of the family during a contingent situation. Their resolve and readiness to respond to the situation are matched by their competence to pick up the pieces as any adult member. It may also be noted that by responsibly handling the situation they have performed two tasks at once. They have not only taken care of a member of the household but also made a tangible contribution to the maintenance of the family. This pattern of children's responsible behaviour is found common in both Coventry and Lucknow.

Domestic work as an instrument for gaining autonomy

Before staking out how children use their domestic work for gaining autonomy it will be imperative for us to know what its essential ingredients are. An autonomous action, according to Dorkin (1989) and Bension (1981), is one which is done according to the free-will and the result of his/her own motive. It is not only regulated by him/her but is critically appraised too, and is redolent of responsibility. It is in this light that children's domestic work will be examined.

The autonomy of children is measurable in terms of the degree of independence. To assess what kind of independence exists and how it is achieved it is necessary to examine what domestic work children want to do; when they want to do it; and how they want to do it. This examination will exhibits the range of their agency as well as demonstrates what opportunity they get for the expression of their agency. Vijay (Lucknow, 15, M) reports:

Vijay: I don't wash dishes. I also don't wash my clothes.
VC: Then who does it?
Vijay: My mummy and my sister do it.
VC: Why don't you do it?
Vijay: Because I do all the outdoor jobs for the house.
VC: Has nobody asked you to do your own jobs at home?

Vijay: Yes sometimes my mummy asks me to do it but I convince her as I undertake all the outdoor jobs for the house and also sit in the the shop.

VC: Which outdoor jobs do you do?

Vijay: I buy vegetables daily from the market... And I do all the other jobs like paying electricity bill, fetching a gas cylinder and doing the shoping.

VC: So, is it because of the outdoor jobs that you do no housework?

Vijay: Yes. Of course. Since I am doing all that (the outdoor jobs) so my mummy and sisters should do the housework.

VC: Do you get anything in return for your work?

Vijay: Not exactly.......

VC: Do you get permission to go out whenever you want to?

Vijay: Yes. Sometimes. Like last Sunday I did the shopping for my house and for the shop. I also sat in the shop for three hours. By the evening I was really tired and bored. I wanted to change so I asked mummy to allow me to visit my friends. She allowed me and I spent two hours with them.

It may be noted that Vijay does outdoor work which is of his choice and also earns time in the company of his friends by undertaking most of his father's jobs in the family. It can be suggested that children like Vijay get freedom from housework whether partial or complete or gain time for leisure only after they discharge their work responsibilities. In another example Rita (Coventry, 15, F) says:

Rita: Normally I cook in the evening but on Tuesdays and Sundays my favourite soaps come on telly from seven in the evening. I don't want to miss them so I have already told my mum that I won't work at that time.

VC: Then who cooks meals on Tuesdays and Sundays?

Rita: Yeah, sometimes my mum cooks and I do my part before seven.

VC: Does your mum allow you?

Rita: Yes. Since I normally prepare meals before seven and that's what she expects.

VC: Do you have the same freedom for other jobs too?

Rita: It depends. Most of the time she allows me. She sometimes says that this should be done just now or at a particular time. Sometimes I do it as she wants but sometimes I convince her to do it later on or do it before. Actually as long as I do my jobs responsibility she allows me. What she expect is [that] the work should be done properly. That I normally do.

According to Rita her contribution as carer is appreciated by her parents and now in the above statements she illustrated how she exercises a degree of choice in the kitchen work. It is the fact that Rita has worked satisfactorily, both in terms of quality and the quantity of her work, which has resulted in her having freedom to do her chores when she wants to and the opportunity to negotiate this. It is to be noted that Rita in contrast to Vijay has succeeded in gaining freedom *"most of the time"*. This is a positive gain over the last example. In another example Raju (Coventry, 14, M) describes how he could trade off the extra labour of car washing for the freedom to play cricket:

Raju: On the last Saturday he [father] wanted me to stay at home to attend the shop and help my mum in cleaning the house. He wanted to take his car for a wash. On that day my cricket match was fixed and I had to go to play at ten.

VC: Then what happened? Could you play cricket?

Raju: Yes. I thought I should wash the car and also help mum in cleaning the house early in the morning so I did it. And then asked dad to let me go.

VC: Were you allowed?

Raju: Yes... he was happy and let me go for the whole day. I came back in the evening.

VC: Do you do it often?

Raju: Yes whenever I wish to have my way I take part of dad's or mum's work. Then they easily allow me.

The case of Dinky (Coventry, 14, F) shows how she manages to have holidays of her choice in return for extra domestic work:

Dinky: Last September my dad had gone to India for five

weeks. In those days I worked a lot at home and also in the shop. Sometimes I also missed my school. When my dad came back from India I asked him to give me £500 pounds so that I may also go for holidays for two weeks to Germany where my *masi* [mother's sister] and cousin lived. At first he was not ready for it. He had spent a lot on the trip. When my mum told him how much work I have done when he was away he agreed to give it to me after Christmas. I could visit my cousin in Germany.

The traits common to all the instances are that a certain degree of freedom is achieved only on the basis of extra work and children are fully aware of the value of their work which they trade off to their advantages. It is not to infer from the above examples that children escape from the parental control, but this is at least evident that they are engaged in negotiating some degree of freedom which helps them to redefine the boundaries of the childhood. The examples indicate growing degrees of freedom achieved starting from partial to a considerable amount. The path of negotiation shows that the degree to which additional work is deemed substantial and qualitatively as good as that of adults the extent of autonomy is realised by children.

Deconstructing the children's statements show that the path of negotiation is not straight forward but sinuous and attempts to exercise agency often come up against barriers. These limitations take the form of established cultural practices or power relationships in the hierarchical order in the family. This is particularly the case for children in the Indian families who find it hard or sometimes even impossible to cross the limits set by specific cultural norms. As Pinky (Lucknow, 14, F) demonstrates:

Pinky: Yesterday I had to go to my friend's house in the evening. My mummy asked me not to go at the time but to sit with my *chachi* [father's brother's wife] who had come with my counsins. My papa and *bhaiya* [Brother] were in the shop. So I had no option but to stay at home and sit with my *chachi* .

VC: How did you take your mummy's order?

Pinky: I didn't like it but what could I do?

VC: Why did your mother stop you?

Pinky: My *chachi* was visiting us. And nobody was there to escort me.

VC: Why can't you go alone?

Pinky: I can go but it was dark and I had to go a long distance to reach my friend's house. We are not allowed to go alone after sunset.

VC: Didn't you so?

Pinky: I did go with my *bhaiya* when he came back from the shop.

The earlier illustration of Smiriti is an example of the limits to the freedom to listen to music when relatives as guests turned up. The above example of Pinky also shows the limits imposed by cultural norms. According to Indian cultural traditions adolescent girls are not permitted to go out unescorted in the dark. Both the illustrations in this way, demonstrate how far cultural norms impede children's freedom. It is clear from both that the scope for children's agency is limited by the cultural demands of the family. On comparison with the experience of children in Coventry and Lucknow we find that the hold of cultural norms has been found to be more rigourous in Lucknow than in Coventry where parents' position as head of the family often comes in the way by hemming in children's efforts for freedom but not residual cultural practices.

How parent's authority constrains children is self-evident from Ajay's (Coventry, 14, M) sore experience in the maintenance of the house. After arranging the lounge along with his dad some time back he had the audacity to rearrange some part according to his own wish and this was corrected by the father again. He explains:

Ajay: After working with my dad and arranging the lounge I thought that the [position of the] telly and audio system be changed. That would look better in my view. So I did it. When dad return in the evening he re-set both as he wanted. I became very up-set and cried. He didn't listen me.

The limitations set by cultural norms and the power relationships between the adult and the child in this way constitute formidable obstacles to achieving freedom. However, despite these blocks children do negotiate some degree of consensus with their parents by making strategic use of domestic work. Mayall (1994) also argues that a consensus between children and adults is achieved through an 'interactive negotiation' process regarding health-maintenance in the family. In our data there are evidence (e.g. above quoted Rita's and Dinky's case) where children as persons negotiate their domestic work responsibilities by exemplary use of the amount of work. The increased domestic work responsibilities of children change the balance of responsibility between parents and children. The change in the responsibilities influences the power relationship between parents and children (Brannen *et. al.*, 1994). The relative change in the balance of power results in an increment of relative independence and autonomy of children. The limitations in attaining freedom and autonomy, however, allow them only to approximate to autonomy and not to achieve it totally.

Discussion and Conclusion

Children's domestic work and their childhood

From the very start it has been noticed that children involve themselves in domestic work as sensible, sensitive and responsible agents. Their sharp observation of family precedes and follows their participation in work. This experience of children is an extension and enunciation of Seymour's (1988) observation that children seem to be observant of adult's behaviour and also appreciate when their help is needed. They not only respond to the call for help but even offer it unsolicited. This is exemplified in the statement of the ten year old Coventry girl who tells her mother to help her father in the shop while she cooks. Despite variations in the expression of reactions to a vast variety of tasks in variegated family systems children's manifestations of a deep sensitivity and responsiveness are found to be constantly present. For example, another ten year old girl in Coventry emphasises that she works because she knows its importance. Her interpretation is that housework is essential for every family and everyone should contribute to it. Another Coventry girl, aged thirteen, explains that the family can run only with the joint efforts of all and says that 'in my family everybody is responsible for some or other work and that's why I have to carry out my responsibility'. Children's explanations of this sort explicitly demonstrate their sobriety and awareness in terms of how they contextualize their work. They have also shown their awareness of the possible implications of this contribution in terms of its desirability and utility for themselves as well as for the whole family.

This study also shows that children are acutely conscious of the conditions and the context of their work. The rigors and restrictions of the power relationship with their parents are well known to them. But according to their age their effort to resist or dissent is perceptibly present. The young ones may submit but the elders as they grow do make their presence felt by raising their voice now and then. The degree may differ: for example Coventry children show a greater degree of self assertion than children in Lucknow. It has also been noted that children have not only given evidence of what is to be done and when but they are also prepared to do their best. They are ready to face the situation and go into it with gusto. If not equipped already they take adequate and prompt action to do so.

Their actual work displays fully how they have visualized their implications and shows their comprehension of evolving situations. Children revealed in the study how, if they did not help in the domestic work and relieve their parents, it could amount to a crisis particularly in the family's health or economic situations. Each ordeal is a ratification of their resilience. They are neither apathetic towards adults nor non-chalant in a novel situation. None appears to have let down their ailing parents or other members of the family. Even when they are suddenly called to stand in they usually rise to the challenge. Pushed into a family predicament they usually picked up the pieces as ably as other family members. The appraisal of their work — routine or in a crisis — has never been found wanting in any respect. Parents of these children have come forward to accept children's work as full work as is evident through the statement of children themselves. Their involvement in domestic work has never been found to be blasé.

The manner in which children shore-up their superiors in varying situations can not be understood in its true light except when seen through their eyes. Their perspectives show their approach to the event and their accounts reveal several aspects of their concerns, attention and application to the work involved which would not be possible otherwise by engaging an outside agency. The incident describing how a very young child takes her grandfather to the toilet is a case in point.

In truth, the children's sense of responsibility, alacrity for action, almost 'adult concern' for the upkeep of family norms and traditions have been a stepping stone towards taking charge of more compelling but trying assignments. This is clear from the examination of assigned and unassigned housework. The greater the challenge the better is found the response in terms of responsibility. The case of a Lucknow girl whose father goes blind shows how, though young, she and her siblings take over on their own the responsible work of the household so that domestic work may not suffer.

Admitting that responsibility is a nebulous concept with different meanings in different contexts, Morrow (1994:132) has proposed that "being responsible involves being accountable, answerable, capable, competent, dependent, reliable, trustworthy and so on". We have applied the term responsibility to involve these qualities. We have already referred above to the fact that in our data children have won the trust and confidence of elders through work in varying situations. What is common to Morrow's study and mine is that children have described a range of tasks which they undertook knowing fully their responsible nature. In her study only some adults 'appeared to acknowledge' that some responsibilities could be passed on to children. In this study we have found that on the basis of their performance children have been given responsible positions freely without any hitch and hesitation which, in a way, is a further finding of importance.

The implications of children's work have been discussed by Solberg (1994). Her study reveals that when children work along with their parents they use their work for negotiations of age and its meanings. On scanning children's version of their use of domestic work, and the meaning they assign to it, it would be apparent that they use domestic work strategically to gain their mediate and immediate ends. Domestic work provides an opportunity for children, as also suggested by Tatum and Tucker (1998) and Sanchez (2006), to gain status within the family. With this achieved status they start negotiating the limits of childhood. Solberg suggests that the negotiation process provides an opportunity to children to socially 'grow'. Examples in this study show how children act as persons and exercise control over the organization of their own lives. Children make use of their work for gaining the bargaining power which they skillfully use in negotiations. It secures them more and more responsible tasks and decision making opportunities such as what should be done and what should not be done. My argument here is that children not only socially 'grow' through domestic work, but by the use of successful negotiations they establish themselves as persons in their own right. Children's position as person is seemingly equivalent to the position of a worker in the labour market where he or she negotiates the value of his or her labour in terms of wages and conditions of work. The illustrations show how they manoeuvre to get free time either in part or, as stated by a girl, 'most of the time' or to have choice regarding their work. Domestic work becomes an instrument of negotiation which secures them more and more responsible tasks and decision making opportunities such as what should be done and what should not be done.

Negotiation becomes a powerful weapon in their hands and is used to define the limits of their freedom. How children have used domestic work to translate their independence and autonomy in practice has been found as a rewarding experience for children in this study. We find that children have seen independence as a function of their domestic work and made use of it to their full advantage. It is interesting to note that Coventry children have different social conditions from those in Lucknow and thus have greater room for independence in domestic work.

This study shows that children get an opportunity to negotiate independence through providing satisfaction both in respect of the quantity and the quality of work. However, it does not mean that the achievement of independence is a facile issue. In fact it implies resolving the conflict of interests between children and adults. This is resolved only when the interests of the two parties coalesce during negotiation.

One strong factor of successful negotiation that has been noted in our study is extra hard work by children especially in the absence of parents. A Coventry girl has stated how she worked very hard for five weeks in the absence of her father which ultimately became a good ground for negotiating for future use of leisure. This leads to an inference that the more children work the more they have chances to gain independence and widen the limits of their autonomy. This probability of the relation between 'a lot of work' and 'autonomy' in the family as suggested by Solberg (1997) is found to be true in this study.

The above discussion clearly brings out that children's initiative and responsible participation in domestic work gives an entirely new image which negates the general concept of the child as a completely impassive, week and recipient member of the family who is involved in domestic work by adults (e.g. Gill, 1998) for training and development purpose (e.g. White and Brinkerhoff, 1981). The picture of the child which emerges during the analysis of the data shows that s/he is a conscious, assertive, sensitive and sensible agent who takes initiative on his/her own agency. The child's responsible involvement in domestic work equips him/her with a persuasive power which secures the desired independence in the family settings. This study projects the picture of children shaping their own childhood through the expression of their agency which contravenes the conventional idea that it is parents as an agent of the adult society who construct the childhood for their children. Domestic work becomes a ground for expressing their forte for agency. It is this agency, which is palpably present, which helps in shaping their childhood.

Children's Domestic Work and The Social Order of the Family

Family is a very significant unit of society's social order. It includes two phenomenon: firstly the existence of a number of persons with interwoven relationships and secondly a fixed pattern of work arrangements. The style of work is determined by the ethos of the family, which is created either by the hierarchical order or else in consequence of cultural obligations, as is specifically the case in Indian families. The distinctive environment of the family consists in the filial ties and the evolving family relationships. How children's domestic work affects the family relationships can be assessed from some examples in this study. A Lucknow girl not only takes her grandfather on a stroll morning and evening but also escorts him to the toilet. This type of work cannot be evaluated without the context because it establishes the conventional family relationship between grandfather and granddaughter. In the example of the Lucknow girl who took care of her younger brother it came to light that she did so because she was the eldest sister in the family. The caring work reflects how cultural obligations determine the relationship between the elder sister and the siblings in terms of work. Brannen has also noted that in Asian families in Britain "seniority is an important criterion for privileged status" (1995:330). We find that in the Indian families in both Coventry and Lucknow the eldest girl works almost like the mother and the eldest boy like the father in the family. This type of domestic work not only defines the relationship in the family but also provides specific status to every child.

The analysis of children's work also reveals that it is an indispensable part of the family's work domestic work order.

It has become clear from the account of children's experience of work, and the meaning it has for them, that everyone in the family has his/her allotted share in the broad pattern of work order, but their involvement in it essentially implies their own actorship. The pre-assigned, assigned, and unassigned categories are the result of children's own image of agency as much as of the parents' system of distribution. Not only that but children's bargaining power and negotiative acumen also determine the ultimate form and style of the work decided. The growing needs of the child along with new knowledge of group-dynamics and personal management and a desire to retain respect for themselves, drives parents to accommodate children in re-structuring of the work order of the family. This interplay of co-existing forces recasts the pre-set work order of the whole family. So far as one member's work relates to the work of another's in a family children's accepted novelties transform the whole family set-up. As such children's domestic work brings about re-structuring of their own as well as others' work. The process continues at times to the stage of refining them too. Children's agency as fully-fledged actors gets a more conducive exposure in the case of children in Coventry than their counterparts in Lucknow. This is probably due to different social settings in the two places, but the potential of agency does not vary on that account.

7

CHILDREN'S DOMESTIC WORK: The Subtle Experience of Gender and Age

Once we theoretically accept that childhood is a permanent social structure it becomes necessary to consider its inter-relationship "with other structural categories like class, gender and age groups" (Corsaro, 1997:293). Children's experiences of work, examined in previous chapters, reveal that gender, age and ethnicity are further structuring factors. It was noticed that children in both Coventry and Lucknow experienced gender and age in their domestic work responsibilities. There was no opportunity, however, during this discussion to explore the significance of this in more detail. It is the purpose of this chapter, therefore, to consider the relationship between children's work, gender and age in more detail.

The concept of gender allows us to understand women's position in the society with particular reference to men. Prior to the development of the greater focus on gender, for Oakely (1994), both women and children were marginalized in sociological research. During the 1970's and 1980's feminist scholars raised questions about women's role in society by developing the concept of gender as a social construction. Although, these scholars succeeded in moving women from the margin to the center of sociological writings, the question of children's position continued to be ignored. The feminist effort, as Alanen notes, "has not disrupted the sociological inheritance of marginalizing children; in discussing gender issues related to children, it has unfortunately, remained just as functionalist and adult-centered in its analyses as mainstream/malestream social science" (1994:34). The concept of gender has not directly been addressed to situation of children. Wherever children have figured in gender-related issues they have been seen primarily as objects of women's experience (Alanen, 1994). For instance, children were referred to in the process of "mothering" or 'caring' with emphasis on understanding women. Eventually, children were treated as objects with needs, translated into demands for care. Alanen (1994) aptly comments that feminist theory has made 'children' into women's 'appendices'. Therefore, in other words, children were used to understand 'gender' rather than 'gender' was used to understand 'children'.

The sociology of childhood raised the 'child's question' particularly in the context of gender and generation. Some authors have specifically pointed out the importance of the study of 'gender' and 'generation' in children's interaction with adults (Alanen, 1994; Brannen, 1995; Mayall, 1996). Mayall (1996) has examined children's experience of gender and generation and demonstrates how children are actively involved in negotiating age and gender based status in generational relationship in the child-care process. She finds that it is children's needs which affect mothers' child-care and shapes it as children want. As mothers perform child-caring which affects families' social relationships so do children affect these relationships through their mother. She also finds that children's experience of child-care provided by parents and other health related issues significantly vary in terms of gender.

Children negotiate their domestic role and responsibilities on the basis of their position in the family which they ascribe by their birth order (Punch 2001, 2003). Children's status based on their birth order is an important factor in family's power structure. Brannen's (1995) study attempts to include gender and the birth-order as factors affecting children's participation in housework. Her study of UK-origin and Non-UK origin children (including Indian origin children) in Britain, finds that the gender and the seniority-juniority (based on the birth order) among Non-UK origin children is expressed in terms of more domestic work of girls and eldest children. She observes that "in practice general norms of fairness were circumscribed by more specific guidelines or criteria such as young people's gender, cultural values, age and birth-order" (Brannen, 1995: 326). Brannen's study indicates that children's gender interacts with structural factors namely ethnic origin, birth order etc. in their contribution to domestic work. Consistent with Brannen's findings, Nieuwenhuys' study of Indian children in Poomkara (Kerala, India) finds that "within the domestic group hierarchical principles are organized, more or less strictly, on the basis of gender and seniority, with very young children and girls at the bottom and adult males at the top" (Nieuwenhuys, 1994:199). These findings highlight the importance of children's experience of gender and age in its cultural context. The studies of Logan (1988) and Nesbitt (1993) on Hindu children in Britain have also found that gender is an important variable in the experience of socio-cultural and religious practices of Indian children.

Looking at the importance of experience of 'gender' and 'age' for Indian children, this chapter examine how and in what ways gender, age and their interplay organize children's work. To do so, this chapter explores how gender and age define and determine domestic work patterns. This is also tend to inquire that do children experience domestic work as an instrument in the construction and re-construction of gender and age? Do children regard gender and age as constraints in their domestic work which are insurmountable? Lastly, does children's experience of gender and age illustrate their agency in any way?

SECTION I

Children's experience of Gender in their Domestic Work

The division of domestic work between men and women has been a long-standing feminist concern (Dex, 1985, Kroska, 2004). Literature on the division of domestic work emphasises an unequal share of work between women and men; women undertake the major portion of housework even when they work in full time employment (Berk, 1985; Coverman 1983; Geerken and Gove 1983; Gershuny *et. al.*, 1986; Robinson 1980; Warde and Hetherington 1993). Gender in this context has been addressed in two ways. One way regards gender as a cause of the social reproduction of inequality. It sees women's work, mainly domestic work, as unwaged work which is not on a par with men's productive and waged work. This lowers women's position in comparison to men's. The alternative conceptualization attributes woman's lower social position to patriarchal society which leads to devaluation of domestic work. It emphasises caring, cooking and house maintenance as an integral part of woman's identity. Women's activities of this type, therefore, lose their social and economic significance. However, both the approaches argue that 'gender' is essential for the organization of domestic work. It is 'gender' which plays an important role in the distribution of household tasks and the time spent on it (e.g. Berk & Berk, 1978; Berk, 1985, Delphy and Leonard, 1980; 1990; Oakley, 1974). Authors have defined domestic work as 'gender-segregated' and 'gender-neutral' (Gregson and Lowe, 1993; Wheelock, 1994). 'Gender-segregated' work is explained as 'feminine' and 'masculine'. Caring and cooking are generally associated with femininity (Poole and Issacs, 1997; Frust, 1997) while outdoor housework such as paying bills, repairing of electrical and household domestic appliances, etc. is associated with masculinity. 'Gender-neutral' work is explained as work equally performed by both the genders. These gender-typed categories of housework are formulated on the basis of empirical evidence.

On the basis of empirical evidence some authors have also identified separate categories of domestic work for children on the basis of gender identity (Goodnow, 1988; Manke *et. al.*, 1994; White and Brinkerhoff, 1981). They find a similar trend existing in the case of children as in the case of husbands and wives. For example, girls' domestic work is found to be closer to their mother's in terms of its extent and nature while boys' domestic work is found closer to their father's domestic work (Solberg, 1990). Authors attempted to list boys' and girls' domestic work and see a child's gender as an underlying condition for the variation of domestic work among children (Brannen, 1995; Solberg, 1990; Goodnow, 1988; Manke *et. al.,*, 1994; White and Brinkerhoff, 1981). Their major argument is that boys and girls gender-based domestic work is aimed at gender-role socialization.

However, studies focusing on gender-role socialization fail to examine the interaction of children with 'gender' in their performance of various household tasks. This is clear from Oakely's study (1996) of young people's attitude in Britain. In her study, she compares the 1994 British Social Attitudes Survey with the Furnham and Gunter's (1985) Survey of Young People, and finds that there is an increase in the young people's share in feminine and masculine household tasks over the last ten years. She notes that the tasks especially like cooking, washing dishes, and ironing are commonly shared between boys and girls. The change in young people's perception and practice of stereotyped gender-based housework is different from adults' (Oakley, 1996). Young people are more inclined to share domestic work than adults. Interestingly, Morrow's (1996) study also brings out the fact that children complain about adults' gendered expectations of domestic work. These findings show that the adult's gender-based division of domestic work cannot be generalised to young people's experience and practices. If young people are found to have established new practices that contrast with parents, it becomes all the more essential to explore how this comes about. It is also important to note that the new sociology of childhood suggests that gender and generation alone cannot explain children's lives; it is their interaction that can explain children's lives in a fuller sense (Alanen, 1994, Mayall 1996). Accordingly children's experience of gender, generation and their interaction in domestic work are explored in the following paragraphs.

The gender based pattern of children's domestic work

Consistent with the earlier studies on children's domestic work the research here also finds that girls do more housework than boys in both — Lucknow and Coventry. With the exception of one girl in Coventry, all the girls have reported a greater involvement than their brothers in the performance of housework. Girls not only undertake more household tasks, but they spent more time on them than their brothers. Their housework mainly includes cooking, caring and house-maintenance jobs. The variation in the extent of girls' and boys' contribution to domestic work is apparent in Rita's (Coventry, 15, F) statement where she reported that she spent twenty to twenty-three hours per week which is almost double that of her younger brother:

Rita: Sanj doesn't do much.... He does little. ....(he) tidies up his room only and sometimes hoovers the lounge. Sometimes he fetches my younger sister from school. That's it..... His work is less than half of mine.

VC: How much time he spends every day for housework?

Rita: ...About an hour.

VC: What about yours?

Rita: Must be double of him.

VC: How?

Rita: Because he doesn't do cooking. He very rarely looks after my sister. I have to do cooking. It takes about an hour. I mop and clean the toilet that he doesn't do. Like hoovering the lounge and sitting room is my job. He never does it. I have also got to look after my sister, but he never does it. So, my jobs are more than him.

VC: Why doesn't he cook, clean the toilet and hoover or

look after your sister like you?

Rita: He is a boy. Even sometimes my mum asks him to do but he never gives any ear. Actually he never listens to anybody and also nobody forces him to do.

VC: Are you forced to do housework by anyone?

Rita: No not exactly. But my mum always tells me to cook and keep the house tidy, because it's must for girls in our families. That's the way our families work.

In a separate interview Sanj, 14-year old younger brother of Rita, confirms his share of housework to be less than his sister's. He says:

Sanj: I don't do cooking. Yes I make tea whenever I want it, but most of the time Rita makes it or my mum ...

VC: What else do you do?

Sanj: A bit of cleaning. Tidy up my room. That's it.

VC: Who does the rest of the housework?

Sanj: Rita or my mum.

VC: Do they ever ask you to share?

Sanj: Mostly they don't....... but whenever I like I do.

Vinni, another 15-year old Coventry girl, explains how she has taken over her mother's household tasks. Vinni's family runs a very busy corner shop with a off-license to sell spirits. Previously her family's shop was only a small grocery store but two years ago they expanded it into a large store, selling a range of goods, especially Asian food. According to Vinni her mother and father both work in the shop and are extremely busy. Vinni reported that her mother's involvement in the shop has resulted in an increase in her housework. Because of her mother's increased involvement she has partly taken up her mother's pervious housework responsibilities. She explains:

Vinni: My mum depends on me because I have taken over her housework. She thinks that I can do all jobs but my brother can't. She always made me feel responsible and that's why I took over the housework. She says, "he [Hari] is careless ..(and) you can do it better" (than him).

VC: What did your dad feel about it?

Vinni: My dad also used to tell me that you are the girl of the house and you should do this and that. I got really desperate. Sometimes I felt like running away for a bit. After some time I realized that it was all right.... (and) I get on with my housework.

VC: Does your younger brother do the same?

Vinni: He does but not much. He sometimes helps me in tidying up. He does a little bit.

VC: Who does the most of the jobs in your family?

Vinni: Of course me. (and) also my mum. But my dad doesn't do much. Hari also, doesn't do much.

VC: Why is your share more than that of others?

Vinni: Since mum and dad work in the shop so we have to do it. And my brother doesn't like to do much then who will do it? So, I have got to do.

VC: What is the good of doing all the housework by you?

Vinni: Now I have a say in family decisions. And my brother has started listening to me.

Vinni's 12-year old brother, Hari, also provides a similar version but in his description the gender based division of housework is much clearer. He says:

Hari: Kitchen work is for mum or Vinni. My dad is not a good cook. Mum is really a good cook. Vinni also makes nice *sabji* (vegetable curry) and that's why she makes it. I think girls cook much better than boys. In my family mum and my sister always do cooking. Very rarely my dad cooks. He hasn't got time to work at home. He looks after the shop and does all other jobs (except kitchen work and cleaning). Mum and Vinni do housework.

These example from two families — Rita's and Vinni's — illustrate how gender plays a prominent role in the distribution of housework and how children experience it. Gender based distribution not only determines the type, the number and the hours of domestic work but also carries the force of the family traditions behind it. Rita's family acts in a partisan way in assigning domestic work mostly to Rita. In Vinni's family the play of gender becomes apparent as her father does less domestic work than her mother and the children follow in their footsteps. It is not only mother but also father who impresses upon Vinni how she has to take up responsibility for the domestic work traditionally as a girl in an Indian family.

The gender perspective argues that the distribution of domestic work on gender lines is underpinned by culture. The cultural expectations lay down domestic work as the sole responsibility of women (Berk, 1985, Charles and Kerr, 1988). We also find that cultural expectations of Indian families generate extra demand of housework particularly for girls. Girls in Coventry reported that they undertake their mothers' housework because their family's cultural practices demanded it. For example Roop, a Coventry girl of age 15, reports:

Roop: In our families [Indian families] boys can get away with a lot more than girls. It really depends on the parents. Like my parents are really strict. It's not a question of where we live because Indian parents favour boys everywhere. My brother, although he's only ten gets favours, I guarantee that by the time he's fifteen he'll have more freedom than me. He'll not be required to do housework. He'll go out to do jobs and that kind of things. ....There are already differences. My brother can tidy up and dust, but he doesn't. When I was ten I was doing all these jobs. My mum used to tell me what to do and what not to do, but for my brother she is not very strict.

VC: Do you mean that you are doing more housework than your brother because your parents are favouring him?

Roop: ....Yes my parents do favour him. But I do more housework not only because of this. Since my mum is not free she can't cope with housework. We haven't got any sister who will take her jobs so I am doing it.

The evidence of Roop's experience displays the force of culture in determining her domestic work. She makes a point that the cultural expectations of Indian families determine children's domestic work along gender lines. Drury's (1991) study finds that the majority of Sikh girls do housework when they stay at home; they help to entertain family friends, look after younger siblings and help out their parents in domestic work. These girls willingly or unwillingly conform to the cultural expectations in performing housework just to maintain their ethnic culture. Drury's study further notes that girls are critical of the fact that Sikh males participate less in housework; they know that their brothers are not expected to do housework because of their families' cultural considerations. Consistent with Drury's (1991) findings this study also finds that despite their desperation with the gender based division of domestic work, Coventry girls consciously and willingly take up most of the traditionally 'feminine' household tasks to ensure that their cultural identity remains intact. In this research there are many instances of Coventry girls undertaking cooking and caring jobs as affirmation of their culture. This is evident in the following illustrations:

Leena: I cook Indian meals because I feel that every Indian girl should know how to cook Indian dishes.

VC: Why do you feel so?

Leena: Since we are partly Indian and partly British so we should know how to cook Indian dishes.

VC: Is this the only reason?

Leena: Yeah! I cook food because we can't live on fish and chips. We eat Indian meals everyday. Indian dishes are our favourite and without that we can't live.

VC: Why is it that only you work in the kitchen and not your brother?

Leena: Yes, he should help us but he doesn't. My family let him free from the kitchen work, but they expect me to do it. If they find me not doing it there is trouble.

VC: So, do you think it is justified?

Leena: No I don't think so. Even sometimes I argue my mum and dad that everyone should share kitchen work. As I think, ...I should do cooking and other jobs. I believe that this keeps our family together. If we don't care we'll certainly lose our identity.

Roopal (Coventry, 15, F) explains why she looks after the family, particularly her siblings:

Roopal: Yes, I stay at home and look after them because I think that it's our responsibility. I think that they need me. I don't want to ignore them like the English. We think, [that] this is our [the whole family's] responsibility to look after each other.

VC: Do you mean that you care for your brother and sisters because it is a practice in your family?

Roopal: Yes, I strongly believe this. You can see in any Indian family children are looked after always by their parents or relatives. I remember, when I was little I used to go to my Uncle's house. I used to stay there with my cousins. They were very kind to me.

VC: Why were you going to your cousins?

Roopal: In those days (my) mum was working in a factory and dad was busy in the shop. They used to send me there.

Leena's and Roopal's explanation of cooking Indian food and taking care of sibling respectively demonstrates that they perform these activities with the explicit purpose of keeping the Indian cultural values alive. Drury (1991) has also found that Sikh girls in Britain still believe that child-caring is the sole responsibility of mothers and outside aid for child-caring is culturally unacceptable. Roopal's comment shows that she critically distinguishes her caring jobs for siblings in the wider context of the British society. It is apparent from her experience that she undertakes sibling care because it sustains Indian cultural practices. So, her dissatisfaction with the gender-based division of domestic work pales into insignificance in the face of socially venerated values of cultural continuity. She appears as a critically conscious agent of Indian culture in the domestic life in Coventry.

Looking at gender-based division of work among children in Lucknow, the study finds that the areas of domestic work for boys and girls are much more distinct and demarcated than in Coventry. Boys in Lucknow report that they never do cleaning, mopping and cooking. In the case of contingency situations they have done such things but this is also very rare. They undertake all jobs for the family which are done outside the house such as buying groceries, paying bills, post-office jobs, buying doctor's prescription, escorting sisters, entertaining strangers, receiving phone calls, etc., while girls are involved in indoor chores such as cooking, caring and cleaning. The boundaries of their housework are clearly defined. The Lucknow girls state that they are doing housework as they are expected to do it. As far as their experience of housework is concerned they do admit to not liking the strict division of housework between boys and girls.

Richa, a 14 year old girl, says:

Richa: My *bhaiya* (brother) doesn't do housework like me. We do all cleaning work and kitchen work but he doesn't.

VC: Why is he not doing the housework which you do?

Richa: ......(laughs)... nobody asks him and he never does. He does shopping and repairing only. That's it.

VC: And what about you and your sister?

Richa: We do all sorts of housework.

VC: Do you think that it is fair?

Richa: No. I don't think so. In fact sometimes I get fed-up with it and I want him to do at least cleaning or tidying up. But I can't force him. Actually here nobody asks boys to do cooking and cleaning.

VC: But why?

Richa: This is the system here. Everybody says so.

VC: How do you like your housework?

Richa: Usually I like them........ (because) I think that we should do housework. After all we are girls and if we don't know cooking and house management then we'll face problems. It's our basic responsibility and that's why I like doing them.

Anuradha (Lucknow, 15, F) explains why boys do not take part in housework:

Anuradha: My brother feels shame in doing housework so he doesn't do it. Even my parents don't want him to do cooking.

VC: Why is it so?

Anuradha: You know, if boys cook meals and girls sit there and do not do anything in the kitchen then everybody will say "What a family is! girls are sitting and boys are cooking!".

VC: But what do you feel?

Anuradha: I feel bad. I don't like this. What's wrong if boys share in housework? We all are equal and if we are cooking and cleaning then why should they be spared?

Smiriti (Lucknow, 15, F) expresses her reactions to the distribution of housework on the basis of her gender:

Smiriti: Last month my mummy was sick for about two weeks. I had to do a lot of housework in those days. I used to wash clothes of my mummy and sisters. I was sweeping and tidying up the rooms. I was not cooking much of the dishes. I used to make *kithchidi* [a dish made of rice] for everybody. I was terribly busy with the housework.

VC: Did anybody help you at that time?

Smiriti: Sometimes my papa was helping me in cooking. Our maid was coming for dish washing and mopping the floor.

VC: What about your brother? Didn't he share the housework?

Smiriti: No. He didn't. He was just doing outdoor jobs like buying vegetables and other grocery items. Actually he never did cooking only he was making tea. That's it.

VC: How do you feel when your brother doesn't share in the housework?

Smiriti: I don't feel good. I always want that he should do some of the housework. But my parents never give him any household tasks. Sometimes I ask my mummy why does she not ask him to share some of the jobs, but she is very soft on him. Even if she gives any kitchen work, like cutting vegetables, to him..... he tries to avoid doing such work and goes away. My mummy never forces him to do anything, that I never like.

VC: Could you please tell me what are the jobs which your *Bhaiya* [brother] does but you don't?

Smiriti: He fetches (cooking) gas cylinder which I don't do. He shops vegetables, pays telephone bill and electricity bill that I normally don't.

VC: Why are you not doing these jobs?

Smiriti: I do but very rarely. I can do it but nobody gives me chance for it. My mummy and papa do not like me to do these jobs.

VC: Why don't they?

Smiriti: I think they believe that girls are not fit for these jobs. Girls can do these jobs but only when there is nobody in the family.

VC: What do you think about your jobs?

Smiriti: My jobs are okay. I think that its good for me to know all sorts of jobs as it is very basic for every girl. It helps us in running the house.

The difference in division of domestic work is confirmed by Lucknow boys. For example, Rahul (Lucknow, 14, M) says:

Rahul: I have never cooked food. This is not our job.

VC: Why have you not done it?

Rahul: In my family boys do not cook so I don't.

VC: Why don't boys cook?

Rahul: Boys have a lot of other jobs to do. They do that. And girls cook food and serve it to all. This is our tradition. Take the example of my papa, he never does it. His responsibility is to bring money and for that he has to work outside. How can he do cooking then? And if he started cooking at home then who will run the shop, how will we earn money? So that's not possible. Normally our mother and sisters stay at home and we go out for earning money.

VC: Do you feel that mothers and sisters can't earn money? Are they meant only for housework?

Rahul: No they can earn money. Many women go out and work and earn money. But even though they are running their families. They can't avoid their responsibility. How can a mother ignore cooking and other household chores?

The above quotes exemplify how Lucknow girls experience gender bias in the distribution of domestic work. Although these girls have expressed their dissatisfaction with gender-bias in domestic work, they did not report any instance of rejection or challenge, whereas Coventry girls, in some cases, do. The similarity in disagreeing with the distribution of domestic work on gender lines and dissimilarity in rejecting or attempting to reject the gender-based division of domestic work in Coventry and Lucknow, draws our attention towards the comparative importance of its socio-cultural context. Girls in both locations have similar experiences but due to the different socio-cultural context the reaction of these girls differs.

Within the Indian household the girl child is generally ranked lowest in Lucknow. The distinction between boys and girls starts at birth. A boy's birth is an occasion of joyous celebration while a girl's birth has only muted reception (Kakar 1981). The qualities that girls are required to inculcate as feminine virtues are self sacrifice and self effacement. This means that they are required first to serve and last to eat in the family (Kakar 1981). The girls are trained to be docile, silent and required never to question their families' decision (Saini 1994). The Indian family structure and values function in such a way that a daughter grows up looking upon herself as an inferior and subservient person (Burra *et. al.*, 1989). She is taught to be dependent on her father before marriage, on her husband after marriage and on her son after her husband's death. Restrictions are placed on her mobility too. As a girl she is not allowed to go about freely after puberty or even prior to it. Traditionally parents try to instill patriarchal ideas into the minds of the girl child. The rural upper caste families restrain the girl child from making her appearance in the drawing and common rooms. Her interaction with male counterparts is viewed with suspicion and a positive relationship between the two sexes seems impossibility (Vasant, 1991). It is obvious from the way the girls are brought up in Indian families that they cannot think in terms of resentment, revolt or rejection of their roles in domestic work.

Of course, there has been some evidence to show that girls in Lucknow have taken over boys work but it is very rare. However, there is no evidence of Lucknow boys performing domestic tasks earmarked for girls. In Coventry, there is more evidence of boys and girls sharing in each others' work. The perceptible reason for this difference between Coventry and Lucknow children is that the Coventry Indian children are exposed to the British socio-cultural milieu. The socio-cultural context of Lucknow children's family is part and parcel of the wider Indian society in which gender is the most powerful structure for the determination of domestic work. The gender emphasis on the domestic work of children is, therefore more prominent and formidable, while the Coventry situation is different. For the Coventry children the family's socio-cultural values still bear the imprint of Indian society, but the social context in which they are living is different. Because of the different social context of these children the force of their family's socio-cultural values gets mitigated to some extent.

Children's agency and 'gender'

The above discussion shows that children perform domestic work along traditional gender lines in both places. The conventional view focuses upon children's gender-based domestic work as a 'gender-role socialization' or gender reinforcement. With this approach it is argued that gender inequalities are perpetuated by encouraging children to take-up gender-specific tasks such as caring and cooking (Thrall, 1978; Gill, 1998). This argument has been developed on the basis of parents' views. In the present study, however children's views on undertaking gender-specific tasks invalidate this argument. We find that it is not true in all circumstances. Particularly, Coventry children feel that they involved themselves in gender-specific tasks to keep their cultural ties intact and alive. For instance, Gur (Coventry, 14, F) reported that her parents do not allow her to go out in evenings. Although she is not convinced by the reasons given for this, she has to listen her parents. On the issue of going out she accepted her parents will but on the issue of housework in the evening she attempts to negotiate the situation; as she reports:

Gur: She [mother] says that going out in the evening is not safe for girls. I don't really feel that this is the only reason. Anyway, its not fair on her part. This is not only my parents do. I know all Asian parents do the same. They have a bit different rule for us. Boys can go alone and they don't mind where they go and with whom. Parents have got to have an equal treatment for boys and girls, but unfortunately they haven't. But I said to them [parents], if you won't allow me to go out I'll do whatever I wish to do.

VC: Okay. Did they listen to you?

Gur: Yes they have to. If they don't allow me to go they have to listen to me. I told them that whatever I'll like, I'll do..... and I do whatever I want to. My dad understands me. He's a bit liberal, but my mum isn't.

VC: Did your brother do the jobs which normally you do?

Gur: Well he didn't want to, but he had to. I said to my dad, if I'm doing these jobs then why can't he, he should also clean the house. And now my dad ask him to do some jobs. Except washing dishes he does everything. But not always..... (smile).

Gur's example elucidates that she is not able to break the gender barrier in going out but she is quite able to negotiate it for housework. Because of her protest her brother does some of the housework. In this way she attempts to confront the gender-based division of domestic work. To some extent, she is successful. Like Gur, Nicky, age 12, also admits that in her family her brother receives concessions in housework. But she aptly describes how she negotiates her gender based household tasks:

Nicky: My mum always thinks that because you are a girl you have to do housework. She was always favouring Ajay [elder brother]. She wasn't giving any jobs to him. She started depending on me for housework. I also get on with the jobs. What annoys me when I find, ... he hasn't got responsibility of any job, whereas I've got to do everything. This is really terrible. ......

VC: Have you not complained for this?

Nicky: Yeah!....One day I told my parents that I'm not going to do all this. I'm not getting time for myself, so I won't do [housework] any more. ....Then my parents realised that he [Ajay] should also do some of the jobs.......Actually my dad is very sensible, he asked my mum to give some of the jobs to him. Now he does a bit.

VC: So do you feel comfortable now?

Nicky: Yes I do. I wouldn't feel comfortable if I kept silent.

Now I'm happy because he does at least something. My dad is of the opinion that everyone should do his jobs..... and that's why everybody has some share in the housework in *our* family.

Dinky (Coventry, 14, F) reports her experience:

Dinky: Me and my mum look after all of them [younger brother and sister].

VC: Have your family ever took the services of child-minder?

Dinky: Humm... no I don't think so. I remember, once my mum was about to call baby-sitter but I didn't like the idea. I advice her not to call baby-sitter and I looked after them.

VC: Why didn't you like the idea of engaging baby-sitter?

Dinky: Because I believe that caring is our job.... I mean, if there is mother or sister in the family they should look after the children first. And I did it........ We can take services of an outsider for our shop, but we shouldn't call child minder for baby care. Ultimately this our responsibility and we should carry out. In case if we can't then we can call, but if we can we shouldn't.....

The above examples explain how Coventry girls are aware of their gender and also how they react to assigned gender-based housework. Instances also show that they tried to redefining the distribution of housework. Gur accepted that her parents treat them differently on the question of going out in the evenings, but her contribution to domestic work makes her an active and assertive member of the family. And through these qualities she deconstructs the stereo-type image of gender. Nicky's example demonstrates that the moment she took over the housework she also began to question her treatment. And to some degree she succeeded in her efforts. She did not deny that her family practices a gender bias; nevertheless her active involvement in domestic work reduces it to some extent. Dinky's example is further interesting evidence of how she advocates the female's responsibility of caring for children in her family. Identifying herself with femininity she undertook the job of caring for siblings. This is not the case of submission to gender-based work, but of reconstruction of gender through domestic work. What is common to these girls is that they are actively involved in the deconstruction and reconstruction of gender through domestic work. It is a different matter whether they are fully successful in the negotiation of gender roles or whether they are only partially successful. They have expressed their discontent and dissatisfaction against their parents' expectations of domestic work on gender lines. This is a cogent proof of interaction between children's agency and structural factors related to gender. Thus, domestic work provides an opportunity to children to exploit their agency in optimum terms and to interact with structures of society.

Gender is also prominent in the experience of Coventry boys. We have already seen in the above section that boys and girls adopt their fathers and mothers domestic role respectively. Here it is interesting to note that similar to girls, boys in Coventry have not simply accepted this gendered based division of work, but the interactions between their 'gender identities' and the 'nature of work' reflect their personhood. Taj (Coventry, 13, M) justifies his work:

Taj: I do all that what my dad does. My sister does all that what my mum does in the kitchen.

VC: Why do you do your dad's jobs and why can't she [sister]?

Taj: I think I can do them better than her. Actually people say (that) boys are like fathers and girls are like mothers, and I'm a boy so I help my dad...... She can't do heavy lifting or so. I think it's me who has to do these jobs after dad. The kitchen work is necessary for her, she must know all that. .....

Raju (Coventry, 14, M) says:

Raju: I don't think it's only me who gets favour. My sister Leena also gets favours. Whatever she wants she gets. My parents always say "She is doing a lot for us. She has taken over the responsibility of kitchen". My mum feels my jobs are less important to my sister. But I feel mine is equally. I did the paint in two bedrooms in last week. I help my dad in every task. Even I take them to hospital whenever needed. My work is mine.

VC: How do your parents take your work?

Raju: It depends. Sometimes they appreciate and sometimes they take it very casual. Mum always take side of Leena. But my dad is neutral. He treats us in the same manner. I think I'm a boy so I have to help my dad and she is a girl so she has to do kitchen work. Why her work is more important than mine. Both of us do equally important jobs. So why's my jobs are less than her's. No matter what I do and what she does.

Ravi (Coventry, 12, M) describes:

Ravi: My mum wants me to stay over here (home); I'd like to go to the shop. My mum says I've got to tidy all the rooms up. She says I ain't going nowhere until I've finished the cleaning.

VC: What do you feel then?

Ravi:....I didn't like her. She kept saying: "You know what you should do, you know what you shouldn't do'. But after some time I felt all right. And now I do whatever she told me. I feel that it's my turn to look after the house. She's is fed up of keeping us all the time.

VC: Don't you think that your sister should do these tasks?

Ravi: Yes she should. She sometimes helps us. You know my family is different. In some families only girls and mums do housework but in my family everyone does it. My parents are not like others who give more freedom to boys. My friends don't do much housework but I'm all right.

Coventry boys' experience of gender is as different as that of Coventry girls. Raju opines that everyone's job in terms of gender is equally important at home. Ravi's earlier feeling was anti housework but as he grew he started realising his role as a member of the family. He does anything that is required irrespective of its gender specificity. In sum, the experience of the two boys quoted above varies with the different set-up of the family. Their reaction shows a subtle understanding of gender.

As far as Lucknow children's experience of gender is concerned the study finds interesting and informative instances in which children react to and interact with gender. For example,

Richa has stated earlier that in her family boys do not do cleaning or tidying up or cooking because of the tradition which prescribes such type of work to be done only by girls. Her reaction is limited to the feeling of being *'fed-up'*. The rigid frame of tradition did not offer her opportunity to give vent to her desire for involving boys in doing indoor housework. The critique of Anuradha, another 15 year-old Lucknow girl, is more extensive as she specifically mentions the social inhibition. In comparison to Richa she is more argumentative for she says *"what's wrong if boys share in housework? We all are equal and if we are cooking or cleaning then why should they be spared"*. Smiriti has earlier said that her parents believe in the division of tasks on gendered lines. They do not like her doing outdoor jobs done by her brother although she done it whenever she gets a chance. On probing further if she was dissatisfied with this she explains:

Smiriti: No. I'm not. But I can't go away. In every family kitchen goes to girls and outside jobs go to boys. For me, every child can do all type of jobs. Look, whenever my papa is out or mummy is sick we all are doing all type of jobs. So, that's not the matter that girls can't do outdoor jobs and boys can't do indoor jobs. All this depends on the family.'

Smiriti's initiative confronts the gender distinction in situations where parents are not available to guide or restrict her. It indicates that gender does not affect her work in special circumstances. However, Namita, another 13-year old Lucknow girl, negotiates on when to do and how to do these gender-specific jobs in the presence of her parents. She says:

Namita: I didn't say no to my mum but I did say that I would do the work the way I like.

VC: Could you explain it a bit more?

Namita: ....Well like my mummy has given me the job of cooking in the evening. I said to my mummy that I will do it but I will not serve it whenever everybody wants. I will prepare the meal and put it on the table. Suppose my Bhaiya [brother] wants to eat any other time then I won't warm it up and serve it to him. If he has to eat he will take by his own.My mummy agreed and now I'm cooking but when to cook and how to cook is my wish.

VC: And how about what to cook?

*Namita:..*Well my mummy tells me sometimes what to cook. But it entirely depends on my convenience. Say... if I have to do other jobs also or I'm tired then I cook dishes which take less time. But if I am free I cook what I am asked to.

Saher (Lucknow, 13, F) describes how she negotiated the order of gender- specific tasks:

VC: Who does cleaning in your house?

Saher: Normally I do sweeping and dusting. I didn't like mopping so I asked my mummy to arrange a maid servant for this job. My mummy said Okay.

VC: So you don't do mopping.

Saher: Yes. I don't do it.

VC: When do you do sweeping and dusting?

Saher: I normally do it in the evening. In the morning I don't get time. I go to school.

VC: Have you never been asked to do it at particular time?

Saher: No. I have already said to her that I will do it only in the evening.

The latter two examples of Namita and Saher refer to routine domestic work specifying how in normal situations too, they seek to impose their will. Namita has her own way of when, how and what to cook; Saher excuses herself from what she does not want to do (mopping) and has her own way even in the order of time when to do her work (sweeping and dusting).

In the above sequence of examining girls reaction to gender the most interesting instance of gender has come to light in 14-year old Lucknow girl Pooja's experience of collecting sugar ration every month. Under the State's Public Distribution system for essential goods Indian government runs ration shops which provide essential items on controlled prices according to a fixed scale of quota to the public. It is common that queues of males are much longer than that of females. This is the context of Pooja's statement :-

Pooja: I go to ration shop to bring sugar every month.

VC: But why only you go to the *ration* shop?

Pooja: You know that the queue of males in ration shops is always very long. Women have a shorter queue and therefore it takes less time in getting sugar. So I do this job.

The above example illustrates that it is not a question of gender being a help or a constraint for children but really speaking it is the manner in which they react to it that brings out their character as such. Pooja offers to do a job that squarely lies in the masculine category of work and does it as well as anyone.

The interaction of Lucknow boys with gender also demonstrates that they have used their gender identity to keep their area distinct from girls. Akshay (Lucknow, 13, M) narrates his experience:

Akshay: I have told my mummy that I won't do cleaning. I am doing my jobs in which she [sister] is not helping me out. Whenever I say that today I don't want to go for shopping then mummy says that you have to go for it as she [sister] can't. So if she can't do shopping then why should I do her job?

VC: What did happen then?

Akshay: I did not have to do cleaning. They had nothing to say and had to do it.

Like Akshay, most of the boys in Lucknow have stuck to their guns by not changing the area of their gender-specific work. This is the normal stand of boys in Lucknow. However, in situations of contingency one 13-year old boy, Ramesh admitted that he did relent a bit. He describes:

Ramesh: Normally I don't do much work I go to buy vegetables and to the flour mill to get flour. But whenever my *amma* [Mother] goes to the village for long periods then I have to do a bit more.

VC: What do you do then?

Ramesh: I make tea, attend to the guests and help my papa in the shop.

VC: Don't you feel then that you are doing sister's work?

Ramesh: I do feel it is sister's work but when my mother is away and guests turn up I feel I should help her a bit... so I make tea.

Ramesh's case is exceptional, however. Apart from what has been noted as a distinctive feature in the reactions experienced by children in gender-based division of domestic work it would be interesting to describe the discriminative features discovered in the two places. The evidence recorded shows that Coventry girls display both deconstruction and construction of gender in domestic work. The line of demarcation between boys and girls has to some extent disappeared through the negotiation process adopted by Coventry girls. They have been able to object to and resist disparity in their work with the result that boys were compelled at times to participate. In Lucknow, girls show a low level but latent discontent and dissatisfaction against the gender-based work pattern without actually questioning these roles. The reason why it can be so fully appreciated when we refer to the Indian social and cultural context of children's housework already expounded earlier in this chapter. It shows how family becomes an enforcing unit of cultural norms and children are beset with double handicaps that are of the family and the wider society. The socio-cultural inhibitions of wider society are so strong that they do not readily permit an attempt to bypass them. What has come out as a piece of greater interest is that although Lucknow girls are placed in such a situation they still given evidence of their social agency which drives them to negotiate the terms and conditions of gender-based tasks. They have negotiated the time and order when to perform a task to suit their convenience. The impression of abject submission and want of initiative does not hold good for them.

The insight and initiative reflected in the handling of gender can be gathered from the example of Dinky in Coventry and Pooja in Lucknow. Dinky uses her gender by choosing for herself child-care. Pooja has made use of her gender for doing boys' work. Both the illustrations show that they have utilized their gender to realize their wishes and do not give up hope easily in the face of conflict of interest between them and parents but with their feet on the ground forged ahead and used all their skills of manouvering the adults. The result is that they mostly succeed in approximating to their end object — social actorship.

SECTION II
Children's Experience of Age in their Domestic Work

Children's experience of domestic work varies *inter-alia* with their position in the age-based hierarchy. Brannen has marked that 'seniority is an important criterion for privileged status' in children of Asian households (1995:330). The general assumption that tasks are distributed according to age of the child is based on the idea that responsibility goes with age. The elders should, therefore, share more in tasks than the younger. Brannen remarks that seniority has particular relevance for Indian families where the concept of seniority weighs more than age. The twins who, may be considered of one age are also distinguished on the order of birth. The senior at birth, by whatever margin, remains senior throughout the life-time. The result is that in between the two the senior acquires a *privileged status* and is always better placed which the society recognizes and enforces.

The significance of the birth order can be gathered from the fact that the eldest child commands as much power as the parents in domestic work during their absence. The evidence in this study brings out that the seniority of children does not remain unchallenged. For instance, Tejal (Coventry, 12, F) describes:

Tejal: I got really angry when my sister asked me to make tea and wash the dishes when my *aunty* came round to our house. I wanted to spend time with my *aunty* but I couldn't.

VC: Why did she ask you to make tea?

Tejal: Actually my mum was away and Roopal was sitting with my *aunty*. So she asked me.

VC: Does it always happen?

Tejal: Yes my sister always gives me jobs. Say, whenever anybody visits us in the absence of my mum she always asks me to do kitchen jobs and she herself sits with them.

VC: Why does she do so?

Tejal: She thinks that being elder she is more responsible and so she behaves like mum. She tries to drive me.

VC: So, do you accept her?

Tejal: Sometimes I do but sometimes I don't. When I don't want to follow her I refuse her. I say that I'll do whatever I'm doing. I won't do extra work.

On probing similar issues with Tejal's eldest sister Roopal (15, F) says:

Roopal: I think the eldest child have more responsibility in the family. My parents expect me to get on with the responsibility of the eldest child, do all the tasks, the cooking, the look after the house and that's it...... Suppose mum or dad is away then who will be responsible. Only I ...as I am the eldest one after them. ...

VC: Do you get advantage of being elder?

Roopal: Yes sometimes I have got it. But I have paid for it. Like my mum always made me responsible for leaving mess around. She says that you are the big sister so you have to be more sensible for all the house jobs. My younger sister is favourite of my dad and she always gets favour from him too. So, most of the responsibility is mine. She gets concessions. Sometimes she leaves jobs and thinks that I will do it. So this is the cost I pay of being eldest.

VC: Do you ask her to do jobs at home?

Roopal: Sometimes I ask her to tidy up the room. I give her some work in the kitchen too.

Roop (Coventry, 15, F) who has got a brother Viv, 5 years younger to her, says:

Roop: For me it's a bit different. I wouldn't be worried if I've got anyone elder than me. I've a cousin who has got an elder sister and she's more free than me. In our families biggest child has got more responsibility. Whether I want to do house jobs or not, but I have to do them b'cos I am the eldest. ....Like if I have to tidy up the lounge whether I want or not. But Viv has no compulsion. If he doesn't like to do that he can leave it. My parents aren't strict for him but for me they always expect that I shouldn't leave the jobs undone.

On asking separately what her brother Viv feels about this situation:

Viv: Yes there could be trouble if she doesn't do the house jobs. But it's all right. She's just after my mum so she looks after the house. She does all the jobs. It's good for me.

VC: Does she asks you what to do and what not to do?

Viv: Yes she does. Sometimes she tells me what to do. I help her in cleaning the house. I don't like to be shouted at so I do whatever she says to me. My mum also listens to her so I haven't got any excuse except to follow her.

Vinni (Coventry,15, F) girl says:

Vinni: Now I don't get so much time to do housework because I've got more commitments at school. I've got to give more time in studies. I've asked my brother to share cleaning. I asked him to do hoover, dust and tidy up the rooms.

VC: Did he listen to you?

Vinni: He has to. Although sometimes he didn't but now he does. After all I'm elder to him.

Vinni's three year younger brother Hari expresses interesting views on sharing of domestic work between the senior and the junior child:

Hari: She asks me to clear the mess, wash the dishes and hoover the rooms. I don't like this. She always says that "I am the elder than you and if you don't listen me I'll shout at you". "You are supposed to follow me" I think that's not fair. Okay she is bigger than me but it doesn't mean that she can transfer the jobs whatever she wants.

VC: What do you do then?

Hari: I don't get on with her. I have massive arguments with her. She shouldn't just tell me what I have to do. Even if she has to give me some jobs then she should give me choice of what to do and what not to do. I don't like hoovering as it takes too much time. I complained my dad that she is forcing me to do hoover which I don't want. He asked me to do whatever you want. So I did dusting only.

Another 10- year old Coventry girl Rajni who has a brother two years older than her, explains how she has broken the barrier of seniority-juniority:

Rajni: I think that in one sense it is true that eldest child get more power than younger ones. In my family too, my brother gets favours from my parents in housework. Whatever he wants he does and nobody says anything to him. I think it's ridiculous.

VC: Have you accepted this?

Rajni: No I didn't.

VC: How?

Rajni: Well today some guests were coming and he asked me to tidy up the lounge and I refused him. Since I went to help my mum in the kitchen and then said to him that "you are not helping mum and you are elder too, so why don't you do it. I'll be in kitchen only. I won't do this. That's it". My mum said it's all right and asked him to get it done.

The above quotes illustrate how seniority gives a privileged status to children in Coventry through their ability issue commands to their juniors and transfer jobs to them. It also displays the reaction of junior children to this traditional pattern. They do not simply accept commands but express their criticism and resentment too. If seniority begets superiority it is assumed that it is good. Roopal's experience demonstrates the fact that she has earned the status to command her siblings to take on extra responsibilities of domestic work. This is a corrective to the general assumption. The senior's position is challenged in several ways. Vinni's and Hari's experiences show that although the senior is unrelenting the junior is quite argumentative and demands choice in the transfer of tasks. This assertiveness and opposition to seniors' authority becomes more evident in the case of Rajni. Her example is not only one of refusal to tidy up the lounge but an interesting illustration of the failure of seniors attempt to transfer jobs. The point to be noted here is that these children have come forward as persons in their own right wherever they get an opportunity and perform domestic work. Secondly, the domestic work also gives them an opportunity to challenge the age-based status within the family. They negotiate their age through their contributions. The process of negotiation evinces not only a change in the shape of domestic work but also in relationship *inter se*. Seniors on the pretext of responsibility transfer jobs to juniors; the same point is argued by juniors as a justification for sharing greater work by seniors and not getting rid of it. This evidence goes to show how junior children are able to express their views and assert themselves to modify the pattern of the commands of senior children in domestic work. The experience of Coventry children in this way demonstrates the weakening hold of seniority in the field of domestic work.

Children's contribution to and exemption from housework in Lucknow, in comparison, depends more on their birth-order. The age-based hierarchy is more expressive in Indian families in Lucknow. It is the position of a member as senior or junior which commands respect, authority, power and privileges in the family (Shah, 1988). Parents are at the top while younger children are at the lower rung of the ladder. Elder children occupy the position just next to their parents. The eldest girl being close to her mother takes over the roles of her mother in absentia; the eldest son who is close to his father takes over his roles likewise. The relationship among children is such that younger have to pay great respect to elders who exercise their power on younger. The Indian family also expects different behaviour from children below 5, those between 5 and 15, and those who are above 15. They are also treated differently (Dube, 1988). In this power relationship the notion of seniority-juniority of children is formed purely on their birth-order and age becomes immaterial. The importance of this relationship is reflected in the tradition of accosting each other. The younger child calls the elder one not by his/her name but by a socially laid down epithet — *dada* or *bhaiya* (for brother) or *didi* (for sister). This custom is not seen in Coventry because of the influence of the host society. The following instances go to show how Lucknow children have reacted to and interacted with the relationship under the stated circumstances.

Renu, a 15 years old girl, tells of how she takes the responsibility of all the housework which was earlier carried out by her elder sister. Her elder sister Mona, 17 years, is now a part-time wage-earner and studying in a college in Lucknow. Renu says:

Renu: Now it's my turn. *Didi* [Mona] is going out. She doesn't have time to do sweeping in the morning........ Mummy says that now you are grown up and it's your responsibility to look after the house.

VC: Does it mean that your *didi* is not doing housework?

Renu: No no. It isn't. She cooks evening meals. In the weekends she does some cleaning too.

VC: Do you give some housework to your younger brother or sister?

Renu: Yes I give them some jobs to do.

VC: Do they accept them?

Renu: Yes they do. How can they reject them? I'm also listening to my *didi* so they also have to listen me.

VC: Who divides the jobs between you and your younger sister?

Renu: Sometimes mummy and sometimes me.

Renu strongly feels that the transfer of domestic work from elder to younger is fair. However, her younger sister Sona, aged 10, is not happy with the transfer of domestic work just because she is junior. She is always ready to challenge her sisters' views. She says:

Sona: Yes they are big but why can't they carry on their jobs. It's not fair. I'm younger than them but it doesn't mean that they always let me down. My *didi* always ask me to serve the meals and water [drinks] to everybody. She undertake all the good jobs and gives me the boring one.

VC: What do you mean by boring one?

Sona: Like she asks me to throw away the vegetable peelings which I don't like. Like she asks me to wash dishes. Like that.

VC: Do you do these jobs?

Sona: I have to.

Similar experience has been expressed by Jyoti, another 10 year old Lucknow girl. She says that her elder sister Pooja, who is 15, gives her menial jobs at home. Because of her junior position in the birth order she has to do as directed and can not reject it. But unlike Sona, she strongly puts forward her views and says that she should be convinced why she is given menial work before she does it.

Jyoti: I am prepared to compromise if *didi* tells me a good reason for doing the jobs I don't like.

VC: Could she [Jyoti's elder sister Pooja] satisfy you?

Jyoti: She wants me to help in everything. Sometimes I do but sometimes I don't want. So I refuse her. She says "I'm elder so you should follow me in all conditions". It didn't appeal to me.

VC: Did you take it up with your parents?

Jyoti: Yes I often did but they say you have to follow your *didi* because she is elder. They also say that it is good to listen to elders and to get to know housework which will help you later on.

VC: How do you take it?

Jyoti: I don't like their saying that I have to do something because I am junior and it is going to help me. I may do the same jobs if I like but if I am forced to do I certainly dislike it.

In another family in Lucknow, Vivek is two years elder brother to his sister Rekha who is 13. Rekha's experience of age becomes more interesting as her gender is clubbed with juniority. Her case is of double disparity, one of age and the other of gender. She describes it as follows:

Rekha: I always cry when my mummy favours my *bhaiya* [elder brother, Vivek].

VC: Why does she favour him?

Rekha: Bhaiya shows off as if he's too much elder. He makes me run about the house for his work when he very well can help himself. Everyone is expected to do his work. Not he! For he likes making me run ...... like bring his cup of tea then take away the cup to kitchen while he puts his feet up! I don't like it at all.

VC: Did you tell it to your parents?

Rekha: Yes I did. My father is lenient to *Bhaiya.* But my mother who favours me also told me to follow him.

VC: Why did they do so?

Rekha: Mummy says leave him. You are junior to him and you need to know etiquette because this will help you in future.

In the case where a child is both junior and a girl what happens is obvious from Rekha's interaction with elder brother. The interesting point is to know how this interaction changes in cases the boy is junior and the girl is senior in the family. This is perceptible in the following case of Akshay who is 13 but junior to his sister Anu by two years. On asking Akshay whether he complied with sister's direction, he says:

Akshay: Not always. Sometimes I do what I like.......... like yesterday some guests were expected and my sister said "lay the table for the guests and serve them". I said no. I would rather tidy up the sitting room.

VC: Then what happened?

Akshay: She [sister] was cross and told my mother. My mummy asked me "what happened? Why are you not listening to her?". Then I told my mummy that I won't do that. Instead I would tidy up the room for them. She said it's okay but go and do it now.

Akshay's sister Anu when separately asked about the issue explained:

Anu: My mummy always takes his side and lets him do as he likes. Like yesterday she allowed him for tidy up the room and not to help us. She says that he is too young. You should understand that he will be all right later on.

VC: What did you do then?

Anu: I felt sad but could do nothing.

The interplay of seniority and juniority in the children of Lucknow presents a different picture. Seniors' commands are found to be irrefutable. In the experience of Renu we find how the burden of seniority passes on from one to another in the hierarchy of age. It also mirrors the spirit of obedience of juniors in general. Of course, Sona as junior resents transfer of selective tasks to her but ultimately she submits to it. In Coventry, there is evidence not only of refusal in such a case but also of juniors' negotiation of the choice of their tasks. The attempt of seniors in Lucknow to enlist constant sharing in tasks by juniors is not always successful. Besides, selective transfer of tasks to juniors is opposed. Juniority does not mean abject compliance and transfer of selective tasks produces strong resentment. This situation is common to both Coventry and Lucknow but children in Coventry are able to negotiate their age whilst children in Lucknow are not able to do it. Agency and the power to negotiate are present in children at both the places because of express resentment. However, because of socio-cultural constraints it has not been possible for children to find a way for its expression in Lucknow as they have done in Coventry where they have negotiated their age.

What happens when age and gender intersect can be understood in two different situations. In the one it is the male child who is senior and in the other it is the female child who occupies the senior position. When the male child is senior he delegates at will; his seniority appears oppressive. The junior who is critical of the work delegated has to do it because he has no option. The junior is not only junior in status by birth order but also by gender. In other words she is doubly minor. In the other case the female child is senior but in that case the junior carries the day and age succumbs to gender. Akshay, in the above illustration, is junior to Anu, still he does not carry out her instructions for housework and gets away with it. Seniority becomes helpless. Brannen's (1995) study also finds that gender relationships predominate over age (seniority- juniority) in children's housework when both sexes co-exist. This supports the fact that the 'eldest girl child... is likely to have to bear the brunt of the domestic grind' (Balakrishnan, 1994: 37).

The above quotes shed a new light on the prevalent notions of seniority in the Indian families at Coventry and Lucknow. The image of seniority does not remain a singularly glorified concept. Seniors see it not as a privileged status coveted by all but not approachable. They do not find it as a natural consequence of birth order. They realise it as a pay-off their efforts required in the family. Juniors have no compulsions to share. The reactions and interactions of junior children also display that they, too, covet the privileges attached to seniority. If they find seniority bearing down upon them too heavily, if they feel it makes them restive they lose no opportunity to speak out against it. Not only that but they use their interpersonal relationship and personal skill to either reject the order or do something else. In short, the children's experience of seniority as reflected in their reactions and interactions gives out an entirely different story. It gives a new dimension to their actual way of contribution to the social order. The claims of one factor, seniority, are disrupted by the logistical factor of agency of juniors who make timely use of it in differing situations.

Gender and age are seen by children as crucial to their domestic work. The experience of children both in Coventry and Lucknow confirms that the allocation of domestic work is based on gender lines. The concepts of gender and seniority-juniority have been pushed forward to them by their parents through the domestic work. The more important issue, for us, is how children have received and reacted to these notions in their domestic work in the daily life. As far as Lucknow children are concerned we have noticed that they have more or less accepted the prevailing notions while children in Coventry have been more critical and assertive in receiving them. In Lucknow, the activities of children are set by parents on the grounds of their gender. Sons and daughters take after their father and mother respectively. Like their fathers, sons normally have to do outdoor tasks which they also opt for and can have the pick of the indoor tasks if and when they like. However, the socio-cultural norms do not permit girls to enjoy this privilege. The prevailing cultural norms in Lucknow steel it as evident from Anuradha's statement — "What a family! Girls sitting and boys are cooking" whereas, the experience of Coventry girls in this regard is slightly different. When gender is pushed to them through gender-specific domestic work they do not mutely accept it. They have challenged and rejected it. In this way, we can conclude that gender shapes children's domestic work more in Lucknow than in Coventry because of the difference in socio-cultural contexts.

Goodnow's ambivalence in respect of gender — 'whether the push for gender comes from the parents or from the children' (1988:15) — is ascertained in the present study. The push comes from both parents and children alike. Gill's (1998) view that it is parents who perpetuate gender, stands modified to this extent in this study. Nieuwenhuys' (1994) observation of social and cultural meanings of age in Indian children is confirmed from children's account in this study. Children's account reveals that the extent and nature of their domestic work is also set by the notion of senioirity-juniority. The senior child is found more responsible in domestic work in both places. Children undertake housework according to their position laid down in the hierarchy of seniority-juniority. Our evidence bears out that age by itself is not all important because a child of 13 who is senior in its family gets different experience of domestic work while another child of the same age who is junior in another family has different experience in terms of responsibility. The seniority-juniority based on the birth order, therefore, provides a privileged status of seniority and also confers authority to command. It is the birth-order of the children, not their age, which steals the lime light.

Looking at the comparative position of Lucknow and Coventry, the study finds that Lucknow children are more inclined towards the division of domestic work on the basis of their status in the birth order than the Coventry children. This, too, is perhaps on account of their socio-cultural contexts. The study also throws light on children's participation in the construction and reconstruction of gender and age. My claim here is that children experience domestic work as an instrument in the construction of gender and age. They are found as active participants in the process more than as mere passive recipients of gender and age. The simmering dissatisfaction of Lucknow girls and outright challenge of Coventry girls against gender specific housework gives tone to their effort to construct or re-construct gender whenever they have an opportunity for it. For example, in Lucknow Richa and Smriti both have identified their gender through housework by accepting their gender role in the family. By way of justifying their domestic work these children effectively legitimize their gender identity. In Coventry, Dinky's preference for looking after her siblings instead of working in the shop explicitly demonstrates her involvement in the construction of gender identity on cultural grounds.

These children have gone ahead in this process. They have used their negotiation power in setting and re-setting their work roles. For instance, Smriti, a Lucknow girl, undertook her brother's outdoor tasks. Her experience leads her to opine that every child can do all type of work. For her, gender should not be a limiting factor. The success of Namita and Saher in Lucknow in modifying allotted domestic work are examples of their negotiation. Namita changes the manner and Saher alters the time of doing domestic work. These evidence amounts to the reconstruction of gender by their contribution to domestic work.

However, children's usage of domestic work in this process is more perceptible in Coventry. Girls in Coventry are more successful in negotiating their gender boundaries than their counterparts in Lucknow. Because of the substantive involvement in both indoor and outdoor household tasks, Coventry girls negotiate their gender and age more than the Lucknow girls.

Children's negotiation process becomes very interesting in situations when gender and age interact with each other. Boys in Lucknow make the most of the opportunity by pressing into service their actorship and flaunting their superiority further on the grounds of age. They opt for outdoor jobs normally and have the pick of domestic ones if and when they feel like it. Girls in comparison do not find themselves in the same position because of the social and family obligations' stricter hold on them on grounds of gender. This holds good for Lucknow girls. The picture in Coventry is different. Both boys and girls are able to negotiate for themselves what they want more easily in the changed family ethos of Coventry. The Coventry girls have a distinct advantage over their counter parts in Lucknow both in indoor and outdoor tasks. The division of domestic work is not made inflexible and the advantage of age to boys does not hold. In Lucknow if gender and age intersect then a boy of younger age is found to exercise more power over a girl elder to him in outdoor tasks. Giving the same gender it is age which determines who does what, the priority being with the senior.

Children's experience of gender and age and their power of negotiation highlight their agency through out the examination. It works in and through the constraints of gender and age and their interaction in the domestic work. We find that amongst children of one family a junior is able to cross over the barrier of seniority through his/her agency. This is a striking point. We have seen that a child can equally well negotiate his/her age in the case of parents too with reference to domestic work. Solberg's (1990) study of Norwegian children has already shown such a possibility turning into a fact. What remains is to explore other areas of children's interaction in the light of their negotiation of age with adults.

Finally, our argument is that gender and age are not the limiting factors of domestic work. They neither include nor exclude an area of work but help in showing how the innate agency of children finds ways and means to express itself through them. This characteristic has been examined in two settings of Lucknow and Coventry. In fact the measure of constraints including the cultural handicaps seen in social inhibitions all reinforce the key idea of agency asserting itself against all odds. In this way, Niewenhuys' (1994) observation that the existing inequalities of gender have failed to stifle children's will to act on their own and contain the agency which enables them to construct their own childhood, has been strengthened in this study.

8

CONCLUSION

Before an attempt is made to draw together some conclusions, it is necessary to stress two important points. First is that both from the point of view of the locations themselves and the social, cultural and economic environment of its inhabitants, Coventry and Lucknow should not be regarded as a case study for comparison. Thus the study does not claim any comparative conclusions for its generalization. However, children of Lucknow were compared with Coventry children to explore the research questions in greater depth. In this attempt some similarities and dissimilarities between Coventry and Lucknow children were noted and explained in their respective socio-economic contexts. The second point is that the size and nature of sample in this study was confined to a particular set of children. As the main aim was to explore a more qualitative dimension to children's lives, the conclusions drawn from this study cannot be generalized. Nevertheless, the conclusions are useful for understanding particular aspects of children's work. Once this is understood, the question of typicality need not affect the weight to be given to the findings and conclusions. It is hoped that this small study of Indian children may provide a detailed examination of the place of children's work in the division of domestic labour.

This leads to the further caveat that since this study is fundamentally focusing on a very specific group of children (i.e. children of Indian origin in Britain) it only provides and insights into the recently raised theoretical questions about children's position in agency-structure paradigm within the new sociology of childhood. It is also to be noted that no small-scale study of such children can establish a general truth, but it can challenge or refute generalities, and this purpose is served by this study.

The discussion made it clear that neither the child labour debate nor the domestic labour debate accredits children's domestic activities as 'real' work; and therefore, children's work in the family does not find any significant place in the domestic labour debate. This gap in the understanding of children's works called for a reconsideration of the concept of the 'the child' and the definition of work. The importance of children's perspectives and of the comparison has been drawn to explore the full meanings of children's work in the family in its wider social, economic and cultural contexts. Existing research on children's domestic work drew our attention to three principal issues: the meanings of children's work, the sources of information on their work and the reasons and motivations for it. However, we have noted that in this body of research children's own meanings to their work has been largely ignored. It is also shown that the factors affecting children's work such as maternal employment, ethnic background, children's age and birth-order, and meaning of children's works in the family was not confined to their own development but has a meaning and significance for the family too. The sociology of childhood has initiated the latest debate where children's work is considered socially and economically meaningful for both the family and the children themselves. In this way, we conclude by stressing the need to look at children's work as socially meaningful and so sought to develop an evaluation of their position within the division of labour.

In the backdrop of theoretical position of the child in sociology, socialization theory was critically discussed. Latest approaches to children and childhood were seen as a consequence of a critical engagement of socialization theory. The position of 'the child' from 'pre-sociological' to 'sociological' child was discussed in order to consider children as actors who were not mere beneficiaries but contributors to societal resources as well. Since there was no definition of work available which sees children's domestic activities as meaningful, an attempt was made to evolve an operational definition of work to cover different aspects of children's activities. To draw the full meanings and significance of children's work the structure-agency approach within the sociology of childhood and the wider definition of work were undertaken. During the discussion the concepts of responsibility, obligation, independence and autonomy were developed as tools necessary for the examination of the meaning and significance of children's works.

After developing a theoretical and methodological background of the empirical study we examined through the information collected from the children the fundamental and substantive issue of whether their domestic activities constitute (or maintain) the domestic work order. Beginning with self-provisioning activities, it assesses them in the light of the enlarged definition of work. The aim was to see whether some of the characteristics of children's domestic activities resemble 'work'. The data revealed that five different categories of children's activities – self-provisioning, house-maintenance, kitchen work, caring and miscellaneous – fall under the definition of work. The extent of children's involvement in these household activities was substantial and amounted to a significant contribution to the family's social order. The examination of children's activities also revealed that they involve a direct transfer of tasks (from mothers to children); that they reduce parent's responsibility for family care and particularly child care; and that they free parents to undertake other economically useful jobs. In this way, children's domestic activities were argued to be 'children's work' which constitutes an organized response of children to the demands placed on them by the family.

We moved on to explore evidence for the central claim of this study: that children's domestic work is meaningful work for both — children and their family. It is further contended that the children use their domestic work for two main purposes: firstly, they define and refine the boundaries of their childhood by the conscious use of their work; and secondly, their domestic work contributed to the maintenance of the family's social order. It appeared that by undertaking certain domestic responsibilities children negotiate their positions and find opportunities to assert their independence and freedom. The meaning and significance these children attach 'to their domestic and care work respectively influenced by their own interests and needs, which are affected by the cultural and socio-economic origin of children and the relationships lived in the families' (Wihstutz, 2006: 77-86)

It was noted that 'gender' and 'age' are structures which interact with children's agency during their work. A detailed examination of these two structural factors in children's work has been done. Children were seen to be negotiating their gender as well as gender-based roles in both cities. However, the difference between Coventry and Lucknow is noted in terms of the degree of negotiation. Coventry children were found to be more successful in negotiating the gender roles than Lucknow children. This was explained on the grounds of the respective socio-cultural contexts of these two sets of children.

The more general conclusion of this study in many ways has been pre-empted by the conclusions at the end of each chapters. It is however, worth providing an overall synthesis of the more general conclusions. In view of the fact that this study adheres to the methodology suggested by the sociology of childhood and the need to study children in terms of the "inter-relationship between the agency and structures" (Mayall, 1996:1). Although the debate in contemporary sociology posits the concept of 'structure' and 'agency' in opposition to each other, there have been a few attempts to examine both structure and agency together for the understanding of social relationships. James and Prout (1997) argues that in the case of studying children and childhood, if we see children as active agents we have to see 'childhood as a social institution that exists beyond the activity of any particular child or adult'. They further emphasize that the construction and re-construction of childhood is to be understood with children's activities within or upon the institutional constraints that it creates. The agenda for research which focuses children's work on a structural framework was designed and the meanings of work were draw upon through children's views. Through this we try to advance the argument that 'children are social actors who are not only shaped by their circumstances but also, importantly, help shape them' (James, *et. al.*, 1998:123).

Against this theoretical standpoint, the present study concludes that there is ample evidence that children in these Indian families are found to be acting in their own right. The data shows that these children's lives are largely shaped in terms of the help or assistance they give to their parents in housework and the privileges they receive in return for this help. Children are found to be meaning-makers. In this attempt their agency finds varying expressions in different settings. This is a significant pointer to children's burgeoning faculties as workers, an awareness that prompts social interaction. Children's involvement in domestic work establishes social relationship. Although the study noted the difference in the agency of children in Coventry and Lucknow, this is not to say that children in Coventry do not have limitations in the expression of the agency. However, there is a degree of latitude which has probably always been apparent through out the examination. The relative difference in the expression of agency between Coventry and Lucknow children is because of structural factors.

From a structural point of view what is of primary importance is the organization of children's activities in the family. This perspective tends to focus on how children deal with the structures imposed on them by adults. The study noted that during the performance of work these children also encountered other social structures, particularly gender, age and ethnicity (in case of Coventry Children). Their interactions with the structures help them in reconstructing their social relationships. What is interesting to note here is that the study finds instances where children by their work not only find new paths for themselves, giving a new shape to their childhood, but also provide new relationships. This also helps in maintaining the social order of the family. This is apparent to a greater extent in Coventry than in Lucknow, where there is a more conducive atmosphere for realization of children's agency.

The dialectical relationship between childhood as a 'structure' and children as 'agents' can be ascertained in the children's accounts in the data collected. Rather than postulating children's work in the family as something against a family's needs, I have shown that the social construction of childhood through their work reflects a different view of what a child, an adult and their relationship is. It has also been demonstrated that children's work in the family is not the result of a particular pattern of family's needs, but is the result of an interaction of children's agency in response to the family's need and the demand for labour imposed by the family on children.

The analysis of children's work explored the ways in which the construction of the boundaries of childhood are entwined and submerged within the specific socio-cultural ideas of Indian families. Revelations of children's negotiation in undertaking the domestic work break with the pattern of work provided by adults and leads to a reconstruction of the boundaries of childhood. In this way, children's domestic activities are substantial contributions to households in the same way as adults make sense of their social worlds. Thus, the argument is that if children's work positioned them in the structural constraints of family and other social structures (e.g. gender, age, and ethnicity) it also creates a space within these structures that cannot always be anticipated without knowing the meanings of children's work from themselves.

BIBLIOGRAPHY

Alanen, L., (1988), "Rethinking Childhood", *Acta Sociologica,* Vol. 31, No. 1,

Alanen, L., (1994), "Gender and generation: Feminism and the 'child question", in Qvortrup, J. and others (eds), *Childhood Matters: Social Theory, Practice and Politics,* Vienna: European Centre.

Alderson, P., (1995), *Listening to Children: Children, Ethics and Social Research,* Barnardos

Aldridge, J. and Becker, S., (1993), *Children who care: Inside the world of young carers,* Loughborough University, Young Carers Research Group.

Amato, P.R. and Ochiltree, G., (1987), "Interviewing children about their families : A note on data quality", *Journal of Marriage and the Family,* 49 (August) 669-675.

Ambert, Anne-Marie, (1986), "The place of children in North American Sociology" in Adler, P. and Adler, P. (Eds), *Sociological Studies in Child Development,* Greenwich (Conn.): JAI Press.

Anandlakshmi, S., (1990), "Learning to live", *Seminar,* 462, Feb.

Archard, R., (1993), *Children: Rights and Childhood,* London: Routledge.

Archer, M., (1996), *Culture and Agency: The Place of Culture in Social Theory,* Revised Edition, Cambridge: Cambridge niversity Press.

Aries, P., (1962), *Centuries of Childhood: A Social History of Family Life*. London: Jonathan Cape.

Asian Business, (1992), Monthly Magazine.

Aziz, S., (1995), *The Global entrepreneur*. Paper to the Conference on researching Asian Entrepreneurship, London, Roehampton Institute, 9 November.

Balakrishnan, R., (1994), "The sociological context of girls' schooling: Micro perspectives from the slums of Delhi", *Social Action*, Vol. 44, July-September, 27-38.

Ballard, R. and Ballard, C., (1977), "The Sikhs: the development of South Asian settlement in Britain", in J. Watson (ed.), *Between Two Cultures*, Oxford: Blackwell.

Ballard, C., (1979), "Conflict, Continuity and Change Second-Generation South Asians", in V.S. Khan (ed) *Minority Families in Britain*, London: MacMillan Press

Ballard, R., (1983), "Emigration in a Wider Context", *New Community*.

Ballard, R., (1990), "Migration and Kinship", in Colin Clarke (ed.), *South Asian Overseas*, Cambridge University Press.

Ballard, R.(1994) "Introduction' in R. Ballard", (ed.), *Desh Pardesh: The South Asian Presence in Britain*, London: Hurst & Company.

Barret, G.A., Jones, T.P. and McEvoy, D., (1996), "Ethnic Minority Business: Theoretical Discource in Britain and North America", *Urban Studies*, Vol. 33, No. 4-5, pp. 783-809.

Becker, S., Aldrige, J. And Dearden, C., (1998), *Young Carers and their Families*, Oxford, Blackwell Science.

Benin, M.H. and Edwards, D.A., (1990), "Adolescents' chores: The Difference between dual- and single-earner families", *Journal of Marriage and the Family*, Vol. 52, pp. 361-373.

Bension, P. (1991) "Autonomy and Oppressive Socialization", *Social Theory and Practice*, Vol. 17, No. 3, pp. 385-408.

Berk, R.A. and Berk, S.F., (1978), *Labor and leisure at home: content and organization of the household day*, Baverly Hills, CA: Sage.

Berk, S.F., (1985), *The Gender Factory: The appropriation of work in American households*, New York: Plenum Press.

Bhachu, P., (1986), *Twice Migrants*, Tavistock Publications.

Bhattacharjee, S., (1990), "Motherhood in Ancient India", *Economic and Political Weekly*, WS 50-57.

Bhatti, G., (1994), *Asian Children at home and at school: An ethnographic study*, PhD thesis, The Open University.

Bhave, S., (1988), *Pan on Fire: Eight Dalit Women Tell Their Story*, New Delhi : Indian Social Institute.

Bierman, K.and Schwartz L., (1986), "Clinical Child Interviews: Approaches and Development Considerations", in *Child and Adolescent Psychotherapy*, Vol. 3, No. 4.

Blackman, S.J., (1995), *Youth: Positions and Oppositions*, Aldershot: Avebury.

Blair, S.L., (1992a), "Children's participation in household labour: Socialization versus the need for household Labor", *Journal of Youth and Adolescence*, Vol. 21, pp. 241-58.

Blair, S.L., (1992b), "The sex-typing of children's housework labor: Parental influence on daughters' and sons' housework", *Youth and Society*, 24, pp. 178-203.

Borland, M., Laybourn, A., Hill, M. and Brown, J. (1998), *Middle Childhood: The Perspectives of Children and Parents*, London: Jessica Kingsley Publishers.

Borooah V. K. and Hart, M., (1999), "Factors affecting self-employment among Indian and Black Carribean Men in Britain", *Small Business Economics*, Vol, 13, pp. 111-129.

Bowless and Gittins, (1976), *Schooling in Capitalist America*, London: Routledge and Kegan Paul.

Boyden, J., Ling, B. and Myers, W., (1998), *What Works for Working children*, UNICEF and Radda Barnen, Sweden: Save the Children Sweden.

Brannen, J., (1995), "Young People and their Contribution to Household Work", *Sociology*, Vol. 29, No. 2, pp. 317-338.

Brannen, J. and O'Brien, J., (1995), "Childhood and the Sociological Gaze: Paradigms and Paradoxes", *Sociology*, Vol. 29, No. 4.

Brannen, J., Dodd, K., Oakley, A. And Storey, P., (1994), *Young People, Health and Family Life*, Buckingham, Open University Press.

Burgess, R.G., (1984), *The Research Process in Educational Settings: Ten Case Studies*, London: Falmer Press.

Burgess, R.G., (1988), "Conversations with a Purpose", in *Studies in Qualitative Methodology*, (ed.), *Burgess*, Vol. 1, Jai Press.

Burgess, R.G., (1989), *The Ethics in Educational Research*, London: Falmer Press.

Burgess, R., (1990), *In the field: An Introduction to field Research*, 4th impression. London: George Allen and Unwin.

Burman, E., (1996), "Local, Global or Globalised: Child Development and International Child Rights Legislation", *Childhood,* Vol. 3, No. 1, pp. 45-66.

Burra, N., (1995), *Born to Work,* Delhi: Oxford University Press.

Burra, N. *et. al.,* (1989), *The Lesser Child: The Girl in India,* New Delhi: Ministry of Human Resource Develeopment.

Butler, I. and Williamson, H., (1994), *Children Speak: Children, Trauma and Social Work,* Longman.

Butler, I. and Williamson, H., (1996), "Safe'? Involving Children in Child Protection" in I. Butler and I. Shaw (eds.), *A Case of Neglect*? Aldershot: Avebury

Cain, M., (1982), "Perspectives on family and fertility in developing countries", *Population Studies,* Vol. 7, No. 3.

Caldwell, J. *et. al.,* (1984), "The changing nature of family labour in rural and urban Bangladesh: Implications for fertility Transition", *Canadian Studies in Population,* Vol. 11, pp. 165-198.

Carraher, T.N., (1986), "From drawing to buildings: Working with mathematical scales", *International Journal of Behavioural Development,* 9, pp: 526-544.

Cater, J. and Jones, T.P., (1978), "Community, Ethnicity and Class among South Asians in Britain", in a paper presented to the conference on South Asian Overseas, Mansfield College, Oxford, 26-27 March 1987.

Charles, N. and Kerr, Marion, (1988), *Women and the Families,* Manchester: Manchester University Press.

Clausen, J.A., (1968), "The History of Socialization Studies", in Clausen, J.A. (ed.), *Socialization and Society,* New York: Little Brown.

Corsaro, W., (1988), "Routines in the peer Culture of American and Italian Nursery School Children", *Sociology of Education,* Vol. 61, pp. 1-14.

Corsarso, W.A., (1997), *The Sociology of Childhood,* Thousand Oaks: Pine Forge Press.

Corsaro, W. And Streeck, J., (1986), "Studying Children's Worlds: Methodological Issues", in Cook-Gumperz, J., Corsaro, W. and Streeck, J. (eds.), *Children's Worlds and Children's Language,* Berlin: Mouton de Gruyter.

Coverman, S., (1983), "Gender, Domestic Labor Time and Wage

Ineqality", *American Sociological Review*, 48, 623-37.

Crowley, A., (1996), "Whose life is it anyway?" in Ian Butler and Ian Shaw (eds.), *A Case of Neglect?*, Aldershot: Avebury.

Das, Mina, (1988), *Nishtha — Our experience in organising women*, in the report on State Level Workshop on the girl child, Unicef, East India Office, 20-22 (mimeograph)

Dasen, P., (1980), "Psychological Differentiation and Operational Development", *Newsletter of Laboratory of Comparative Human Development*, 2, pp. 82-86.

Delphy, C. and Leonard, D., (1992), *Familiar Exploitation*, Cambridge: Polity Press

Denzin, N.K., (1977), *Child Socialization*, London: Macmillan.

Dodson, Lisa and Dickert, Jillian, (2004), "Girls' family labour in low-Income households: A decade of qualitative research", *Journal of Marriage and Family*, Vol. 66, May, pp. 318-332.

Dreitzel, P., (1973), "Childhood and Socialization", London: Macmillan.

Drury, B., (1991), "Sikh Girls and the Maintenance of an Ethnic Culture", *New Community*, Vol. 17, No. 3, pp. 387-399.

Dube, L., (1981), "The Economic Roles of Children in India: Methodological Issues", in G. Rodgers and and G. Standing (eds), *Child Work, Poverty and Underdevelopment*, Geneva: ILO, pp. 179-213.

Dube, L., (1988), "On the Construction of Gender in India, Hindu Girls in Patrilineal India", *Economic and Political Weekly*, 30 April: WS11-WS24.

Dworkin, G., (1989), "The concept of Autonomy", in John Christman, ed. in *The Inner Citadel: Essays on Individual Autonomy*, NewYork: Oxford University Press.

Dex, S., (1985), *The Sexual Division of work: Conceptual Revolutions in the Social Sciences*, Harvester.

Editors, (1999), "Editorial: Differentiaon of Childhood", *Childhood*, Vol. 6, No. 2, pp. 163-6.

Eisenberg, N., Lundy, T., Shell, R., and Roth, K., (1985), *"Children's justifications for their adult and peer-directed complaint behaviors"*, *Developemental Psychology*, 21, pp. 325-331.

Elder, G., (1974), *Children of the Great Depression*, Chicago: University of Chicago Press.

Ethnic Minority Business Service, *Newsletter*, (1992), Oxford.

Farver, J. and Howes, C., (1988), "Cross-cutural Differences in Social

Interaction: A comparison of American and Indonesian Children", *Journal of Cross Cultural Psychology*, Vol. 19, No. 2, 203-215.

Finch, J., (1989), *Family Obligations and Social Change*. Cambridge: Polity Press.

Finch, J. and Mason, J., (1993), *Negotiating Family Responsibilities*. London: Routledge.

Fontana, A. and Frey, J.H., (1994), "Interviewing—The Art of Science", in N.Denzin and Y. Lincoln (eds), *Handbook of Qualitative Research*, Thousand Oaks: Sage.

Frederiksen, L., (1999), "Child and Youth Employment in Denmark: Comments on children's work from their own perspective", *Childhood*, Vol. 6, No. 1, pp. 101-112.

Fürst E.L., (1997), "Cooking and Feminity", *Women's Studies International Forum*, Vol. 20, No. 3, pp. 441-449.

Fyfe, A., (1989), *Child Labour*, Cambridge: Polity Press

Garbarino. J., Scott, F. M. and Erikson Institute, (1992), *What Children Can Tell Us*, San Francisco: Jossey-Bars.

Gardiner, J., (1995), *New Thinking on the Domestic Labour*, Research Working Paper 11, Gender Analysis and Policy Unit, University of Leeds.

Geerken, M. and Gove, W., (1983), *At Home and At Work: The Family's Allocation of Labour*, Beverly Hills: Sage.

George, I., (1990), *Child Labour and Child Work*, New Delhi: Ashish Publishing House.

Gershuny J.I., Miles, I., Jones, S., Mullins, C., Thomas, G. and Wyatt, S.M.E., (1986), "Preliminary Analysis of the 1983/4 ESRC Time Budget Data", *Quarterly Journal of Social Affairs*, 2, 13-39.

Giddens, A., (1979), *The Central Problems of Social Theory*, London: Macmillan.

Gill, G. K., (1998), "The strategic involvement of children in housework: An Australian case of two-income families", *The International Journal of Comparative Sociology*, Vol. 39, No. 3, pp. 301-314.

Gittins, D., (1998), *The Child in Question*, Basingstoke: Macmillan.

Glence, E.N., (1983), "Split houshold, small producer and dual wage earner: an analysis of Chinese-American family Strategies", *Journal of Marriage and the Family*, Vol. 45, No. 1.

Goldscheider, F.K. and Waite, L.J., (1991), *New families, no families:*

The transformation of the American home, Berkeley: University of California Press.

Goldstein, B. and Oldham, J., (1979), "Children and Work: A Study of Socialization", *New Brunswick*, NJ: Transaction Books.

Goodnow, J.J., (1988), "Children's household work: Its nature and functions", *Psychological Bulletin*, 103

Goodnow J. and Delaney, S., (1989), "Children's household work: Differentiating types of work and style of assignment", *Journal of Applied Development Psychology*, Vol. 10, 209-226.

Greenberger, E. and Steinberg, L.D., (1986), *When Teenagers Work*, New York: Basic Books.

Gregson, N. and Lowe, M., (1993), "Renegotiating the domestic division of labour? A study of dual career households in north east and south east England", *Sopciological Review*, Vol. 41, pp. 475-505.

Grint, (1998), *The Sociology of Work: An Introduction*, Second Edition, Cambridge: Polity Press.

Grusec, J.E., (1982), "The socialization of altruism", in N. Eisenberg-Berg (ed), *The Development of Prosocial Behaviour*, New York: Academic Press.

Grusec, J.E., (1985), *Mediators of parental responses to prosocial behavior*, Paper presented at the biennial meeting of the International society for Behavioral Development, Tours, France.

Gullestad, M., (1984), "Children's Care for Children", *Social Analysis*, Vol. 23, (8) pp. 38-52.

Hammersley, M. and Atkinson, P., (1995), *Ethnography: Princple in Practice*, Second Edition, London: Routledge

Hardman, C., (1973), "Can there be an Anthropology of children"? *Journal of the Anthropological Society of Oxford*, Vol. 4:1.

Hedges J. N. and Barnett, J.K., (1972), "Working women and the division of household tasks", *Monthly Labour Review*, 95 (January): 9-14

Helweg, A., (1986), *Sikhs in England, London*, Oxford University Press.

Hendrick, H., (1990), "Constructions and Reconstructions of British Childood: An Interpretive Survey, 1800 to the present", in A. James and A. Prout (eds.), *Constructing and Reconstructing Childhood*, London: Falmer Press.

Hill, M., Laybourne, A. and Borland, M., (1996), "Engaging with Primary-aged Children about their Emotion and Well-being: Methodological Consideration", *Children and Society*, Vol. 10, No. 2.

Hill, M., (1992), "Children's Role in the Domestic Economy", *Journal of Consumer Studies and Home Economics*, Vol. 16.

Hobbs, S. and McKechnie, J., (1997), *Child Employment in Britain*, London: The Stationary Office.

Hofferth, S.L. and Sandberg, J.F., (2001), "How American Children use their Time", *Journal of Marriage and Family*, Vol. 63, 295-308.

Hood, S., Kelly, P. and Mayall, B., (1996), "Children as Research Subjects: A Risky Enterprise", *Children and Society*, Vol. 10, No. 2.

Hughes, C., (1992), "A Stranger in the House", *Reseaiching the Step Family* in *Qualitative Methodology*, Vol. 3, London: JAI Press.

Hughes, C., (1989), *An Ethnographic Study of the Step Family*, PhD Thesis, Department of Sociology, University of Warwick.

Inkeles, E., (1968), "Society, Social Structure and Child Socialization", in J.A. Clausen (ed.), *Socialization and Society*, Boston: Little, Brown and Company.

Jackson, B. and Gravey, A., (1974), "The Chinese Children of Britain", *New Society*, 3, October.

Jackson, R. and Nesbitt, E., (1993), *Hindu Children in Britain*, Stoke on Trent: Trentham.

James, A. and Prout, A., (1990), *Constructing and Reconstructing Childhood*, First Edition, London: Falmer.

James A. and Prout, A., (eds) (1997a), *Constructing and Reconstructing Childhood*, Second Edition, London: Falmer.

James A. and Prout, A., (eds) (1997b), "Preface to second edition", *Constructing and Reconstructing Childhood*, Second Edition London: Falmer.

James, A., Jenks, C. and Prout, A., (1998), *Theorising Childhood*, Cambridge: Polity Press.

James, G.J., (1974), *Sikh Children in Britain*, London: Oxford University Press.

Jennifer, P., (1988), "What can Case Studies Do? in *Studies in Qualitative Methodology* (ed) Burgess, Vol. 1.

Jenks, C., (Ed) (1982), *The sociology of childhood—Essential Readings*, London: Batsford.

Jenks, C., (1996), *Childhood*, London : Rotledge.

Jones T., McEvoy, D., and Barret, G., (1994), "Raising capital for the ethnic minority small firm", in Hughes, A. and Storey,

D.J., *Finance and Small Firm,* London: Routledge.

Jones, T., (1982), "Small business development and the Asian Community in Britain", *New Community,* Vol. 9 (3)

Kakar, S., (1981), *The Inner World: A Psychoanalytic Study of Childhood and Society in India,* New Delhi: Oxford University Press.

Kallarackal, A.M. and Herbert, M., (1976), "The happiness of Indian Immigrant Children", *New Society,* Vol. 35, 699, 26 Feb., 422-424.

Kanitkar, S.D., (1996), "Gender discrimination in the family: Views and experiences of teenage girls", *Journal of Family Welfare,* Vol. 42, No. 4, pp. 32-38.

Kosonen, M., (1996), "Siblings as providers of support and care during middle childhood: children's perceptions", *Children amd Society,* Vol. 10, pp. 267-279.

Kroska, Amy, (2004), "Division of Domestic Work", *Journal of Family Issues,* Vol. 25, No. 7, pp. 900-932.

Latury, J., (1980), *Classe sociale, milieu familial, intelligence.* [Social class, family milieu, intelligence], Paris: Presses Universitaires de France.

Lavalette, M., (1994), *Child Employment in the Capitalist Labour Market,* Aldershot: Avebury.

Lavalette, M., Hobbs, S., Lindsay, S., and McKechine, J., (1995), "Child employment in Britain: Policy Myth and Reality", *Youth and Policy,* Vol. 47.

Lavalette, M., (1996), "Thatcher's Working Children: Contemporary Issues of Child Labour", in J. Pilcher and S. Wagg (eds.), *Thatcher's Children? Politics, Childhood and Society in the 1980s and 1990s,* London: Falmer

Laybourn, A., Brown, J., and Hill, M., (1996), *Hurting on the Inside: Children, Families and Alcohol,* Aldershot: Avebury.

Lee, Yun-Suk, Schneider, B. and Waite, Linda J., (2003), "Children and housework: Some Unanswered Questions", *Sociological Studies of Children and Youth,* Vol. 9, 105-125.

Leonard, D. (1990), *Sex and Generation,* London: Tavistock.

Light, H.K., Hertsgaard, D. and Martin, R.E., (1985), "Farm Children's Work in the Family", *Adolescence,* 20.

Logan, P., (1988), "Practising Religion: British Hindu children and the Navaratri festival", *British Journal of Religious Education,* Summer, pp. 160-169.

Luthra, Mohan, (1997), *Britain Black Population*, Aldershot: Ashgate.

Lynch, M., (1975), "Sex role stereotypes: Household Work of Children", *Human Ecology Forum*, 5, 1-5.

MacLennan, E., Fitz, J. and Sullivan, J., (1985), *Working Children*, Low Pay Unit, London.

Maharatna, A., (1997), "Children's work activities, surplus labour and fertilit: case study of six villages in Birbhum", *Economic and Political Weekly*, Feb. 15.

Mahon, A., Glendinning, C., Clarke, K., and Criag, G., (1996), "Researching Children: Methods and Ethics", *Children and Society*, Vol. 10, No. 2, pp. 145-154.

Mamdani, M., (1973), "The Myth of Population Control", *Monthly Review Press*, New York.

Mamdani, M., (1981), *The ideology of population control*, in K.L. Michaleson (ed), *And the Poor Get Children: Radical Perspectives on Population Dynamics*, New York: Monthly Review Press, pp. 39-49.

Mandell, N., (1988), "The least Adult role in Studying Children", *Journal of Contemporary Ethnography*, Vol. 16, No. 4.

Manke, B., Seery, Brenda L., Croute, Ann C. and McHale, S.M., (1994), "The three corners of domestic labour: Mothers', Fathers', and children's weekday and weekend housework", *Journal of Marriage and the Family*, Vol. 56, pp. 657-668.

Mauthner, M., (1997), "Methodological aspects of collecting data from children: lessons from three research projects", *Children and Society*, Vol. 11, No. 1, pp. 16-28.

Mayall, B. (eds.), (1994), *Children's Childhoods: Observed and Experienced*, London: Falmer Press.

May, T., (1993), *Social Resaerch: Issues, Methods and Process*, Buckingham: Open University Press.

Mayall, B., (1996), *Children, Health and the Social Order*, Buckingham: Open University Press.

Mayall, B., (1998), "Towards a sociology of child health", *Sociology of Health and Illness*, Vol. 20, No. 3, pp. 269-288.

McEvoy, D. and Aldrich, H., (1986), "Survival rates of Asian and White Retailers", *International Small Business Journal*, Vol 4, No. 3, pp. 28-37.

McClelland, D.C., (1961), *The Achieving Society*, New York, Free Press.

Mead, M., (1954), *Growing up in New Guinea*, Hamondawort: Penguin.

Medrich, E.A., Roizen, J. Rubin, V. and Buckley, S., (1982), *The Serious Business of Growing up*, Berkeley: University of California Press.

Metcalf, H., Modood, T. and Virdee, S., (1996), *Asian Self-Employment: The Interaction of Cultural and Economics in England*, London: Policy Studies Institute.

Mizen, P., (1992), "Learning the hard way: The extent and significance of child labour in Britain", *British Journal of Education and Work*, Vol. 5, No. 3, pp. 5-17.

Mizen, P., Bolton, A. and Pole, C., (1999), "School Age Workers: The Paid Employment of Children in Britain", *Work, Employment and Society*, Vol. 13, No. 3, pp. 423-438.

Morris, L., (1990), *The Workings of the Household: A US-UK Comparison*, Cambridge: Polity Press.

Morrow, V., (1992a), *Family vaiues: accounting for children's contribution to domestic economy*, Working Paper no. 10, Sociological Research Grop, University of Cambridge.

Morrow, V., (1992b), *A sociological study of the economic roles of children, with particular reference to Birmingham and Cambridgeshire*, unpublished PhD thesis, Faculty of Social and Political Sciences, University of Cambridge.

Morrow, V., (1994), "Responsible Children? Aspects of children's work and employment outside school in contemporary UK", in Mayall, B. (eds.), *Children's childhoods: Observed and Experienced*, London: Falmer Press.

Morrow, V., (1996), "Rethinking childhood dependency: children's contribution to the domestic economy", *The sociological Review*, vol,

Morrow V. and Richards, M., (1996), "The ethics of social research with children: An overview", *Children & Society*, Vol. 10. pp. 90-105.

Morse, J.M., (1994), "Designing Funded Qualitative Research", in N.K. Denzin and Y.S. Lincoln, (eds.), *Handbook of Qualitative Research*, Thousand Oak: Sage.

Mullins, D., (1979), "Asian Retailing in Croydon", *New Community*, 7, pp. 403-405.

Munroe, R. H., Robert, L. M. and Harold, S. S., (1984), "Children's work in four cultures: Determinanats and Consequences",

American Anthropologists, 86, pp. 369-79.

Nadkarni, M.V., (1976), "Overpopulation and the Rural Poor", *Economic and Political Weekly,* Special Number August.

Nesbitt, E., (1990), "Religion and Identity: the Valmiki Community in Coventry", *New Community,* Vol. 16, No. 2, pp. 261-274.

Nesbitt, E., (1993), "Gender and Religious Traditions: the Role-Learning of British Hindu Children", *Gender and Education,* Vol. 5. No. 1, pp. 81-91.

Nesbitt, E., (1995), "Punjabis in Britain: Cutural History and Cultural Choices", *South Asia Research,* Vol. 15, No. 2, pp. 221-240.

Nesbitt, E., (2000), "Researching 8 to 13-years olds' Perspectives on their Experience of Religion", in Lewis, A. And Lindsay, (eds), G. *Reseraching Children's Prespectives,* Buckingham: Open University Press.

Nieuwenhuys, O., (1994), *Children's Lifeworlds, Gender, Welfare and Labour in the Developing World,* London: Routledge.

Nieuwenhuys, O., (1995), "The domestic economy and the exploitation of children's work: The case of Kerala", *The International Journal of Children's Right,* Vol. 3, 213-225

Nuttall, E., Chieh, L. And Nuttall, R., (1988), "Views of the family by Chinese and U.S. Children : A comparative study of kinetic family drawings", *Journal of School Psychology,* Vol. 26, No. 2, pp. 191-194.

O'Brien, M., (1995), "Allocations of Resources in Households: Children's Perspectives", *Sociological Review,* Vol. 43, 3, pp. 501-17.

O'Brien, M., Alldred, P. and Jones, D., (1996), "Children's construction of family and kniship", in J. Brannen and M. O'Brien, London: Falmer Press.

O'Donnell, C. and White, L., (1998), *Invisible hands: Child Employment in North Tyneside,* London: Low Pay Unit.

Oakely, A., (1974), *The Sociology of Housework,* London: Robertson.

Oakely, (1994), "Women and Children First and Last: Parallels and Differences between Children's and Women's Studies", in B. Mayall (ed.), *Children's Childhoods : Observed and Experienced,* London: Falmer Press.

Oakely, A., (1996), "Gender Matters: Man the Hunters", in Roberts, H. And Sachdev, D (eds.), *Young People Attitudes,* Illford, Barnardos

Oldman, D., (1994), "Adult child relations as class relations", in J.Qvortrup *et. al.*, (eds.), *Childhood Matters, Social Theory, Practice and Politics,* Aldershot: Avebury.

OPCS, (1993), *1991 Census: Ethnic Group and Country of Birth, Great Britain,* Vol. 2.2, London: HMSO.

Owen, D., (1995), *Ethnic Minorities in Great Britain: Economic Characteristics 1991,* Statistical Papers, National Ethnic Minority Data Archive, CRER, University of Warwick.

Pahl, R.E., (1984), *Divisions of Labour,* Oxford: Blackwell.

Parsons T., (1951), *The Social System,* London: Routledge and Kegan & Paul.

Patton, M.Q., (1990), *Qualitative Evaluation and Research Methods,* Second edition, Newbury Park CA: Sage.

Pettitt, B., (1998), "Introduction", in B. Pettitt, *Children and work in the UK: Reassessing the Issues,* London: Child Poverty Action Group.

Phizacklea, A., (1988), "Entrepreneurship, Ethnicity and Gender", in Westwood, S. and Bhachu, P. (eds.), *Enterprising Women,* London: Routledge.

Pinto, A., Folkers, E. and Sines, J., (1991), "Dimensions of Behavior and Home Environment in School-Age Children: India and the United States", *Journal of Cross-Cultural Psychology,* Vol. 22, No. 4, pp. 491-508.

Pole, C., Bolton, A. and Mizen, P., (1999), *Realising Children's Agency in Research: Partners and Participants?*

Pond, C. and Searle, A., (1991), *The Hidden Army: Children at Work in the 1990s,* L.P.U. London.

Poole, M. and Issacs, D., (1997), "Caring: A gendered Concept", *Women's Studies International Forum,* Vol. 20, No. 4, pp. 529-536.

Price Williams, D., Gordon, W., and Ramirez, N., (1969), "Skill and Conservation: A Study of Pottery Making Children", *Developmental Psychology,* 1, 769.

Propper, A.M., (1972), "The Relationship of Maternal Employment to Adolescent Roles, Activities, and Parental Relationships", *Journal of Marriage and the Family,* 34, pp. 417-421.

Prout, A., (1987), "An analytical Ethnography of Sickness Absence in an English Primary School", Unpublished Ph.D. thesis, *Center for Medical Social Anthropology,* University of Keele, Staffordshire, England.

Prout, A. and James, A., (1997), "A new paradigm for the sociology of childhood? Provenance, Promise and Problems", in James, A and Prout, A. (eds.), *Constructing and Reconstructing Childhood*, Second Edition, London: Falmer Press.

Pugsley, Coffey and Delamont, (1996), "I don't eat peas anyway! Classroom stories and the social construction of childhood", in I. Butler and I. Shaw (eds.), *A Case of Neglect?* Aldershot: Avebury.

Punch, S., (2001), "Household division of labour: Generation, Gender, Age, Birth Order and Sibling Composition", *Work, Employment and Society*, 15, 4,, 803-823.

Punch, S., (2003), "Childhoods in the Majority World: Miniature Adults or Tribal Children?", *Sociology*, 37, 2, 277-295.

Qvortrup, J., (1985), "Placing Children in the Division of Labour", in Close, P. and Collins, R. (eds.), *Family and Economy in Modern Society*, Macmillan Press, London.

Qvortrup, J., (1987), "Introduction", *International Journal of Sociology*, Vol. 17 (3), Special Issue "The Sociology of Childhood".

Qvortrup, J., (1994a), "Childhood Matters: an Introduction" in J. Qvortrup, M. Bardy, G. Sgritta and H. Wintersberger (eds.), *Childhood Matters*, Aldershot: Avebury.

Qvortrup, J., (1994b), "A New Solidarity Contract?", in Qvortrup *et. al.*, (eds.), *Childhood Matters*, Aldershot: Avebury.

Qvortrup, J., Bardy, M., Sgritta, G., and Wintersberger, H. (eds) *Childhood Matters*, Aldershot: Avebury

Ransom, P., (1998), *Work Paradigm.*

Reynolds, P.. (1991), Child Labour in the Zambezi Valley, Harare: Baobab Books with Zed Press Ltd.

Robinson, V., (1990), "Boom and Gloom: the Success and Failure of South Asians in Britain", in Colin Clarke and others (eds.), *South Asian Overseas*, Cambridge: Cambridge University Press.

Rogers, G. and Standing G. (eds), (1981), *Child Work, Poverty and Underdevelopment*, Geneva: ILO.

Sanchez, Martha Areli Ramirez, (2006), "Helping at Home: The Concept of Childhood and Work Among the Nahuas of Tlaxcala, Mexico", in Hungerland *et. al.*, (eds.), *Working to be Someone*, London: Jessica Kingsley Publisher.

Sanders, J. and Nee, V., (1996), "Immigrant self-employment: the Family as Social Capital", *American Sociological Review*, Vol. 61, pp. 231-249.

Saini, D.S., (1994), "Children of a Lesser God, Child Labour Law and Compulsory Primary Education", *Social Action*, Vol 44, July-September, pp. 1-13.

Save the Children, (1998), "Children's Perspectives on Work", in B. Pettitt, *Children and work in the UK: Reassessing the Issues*, London: Child Poverty Action Group.

Schildkrout, E., (1978), "Age and Gender in Hausa Society: Socio-Economic Roles of Children in Urban Kano", in J. LaFontaine (ed.), *Sex and Age as Principles of Social Differenciation*, New York : Academic Press.

Schildkrout, E., (1979), "Women's Work and Children's Work: Variation among Moslems in Kano", in S. Wallman (ed) *Social Anthropology of Work*, New York: Academic Press.

Schildkrout, E., (1980), "Children's Work Reconsidered", *International Social Sciences Journal*, Vol. 32(3), pp. 479-89.

Scribner, S., (1984), "Studying Working Intelligence", in B. Rogoff and J. Lave, (eds.), *Everyday Cognitio: its Development in Social Context*, Cambridge,MA: Harvard University Press.

Segel, J. and Simkins, J. (1993), *My Mum Needs Me: Helping Children with ill or Disabled Parents*, Harmondsworth, Penguin.

Siegert, M., (1986), "Adult Elicited Behaviour: The Paradox of Measuring Social Competence Through Interviewing", in Cook-Cumperz, J., Corsaro,W. and Streeck, J., (eds.), *Children's Worlds and Children's Language*, Berlin: Mouton de Gruyter.

Seymore, S., (1988), "Expression of Responsibility among Indian Children: Some Precursors of Adult Status and Sex Roles", *Ethos*, Vol. 16, No. 4, pp. 355-370.

Shah, A.M., (1988), "The Phase of Dispersal in the Indian Family Process", *Sociological Bulletin*, Vol. 37, No. 1&2, pp. 33-47.

Shaw, I., (1996), "Unbroken Voices: Children, Young People and Qualitative Methods", in I. Butler and I. Shaw (eds.), *A Case of Neglect*? Aldershot: Avebury.

Solberg, A. and Danieisen, K., (1988), *Dagiliglivetes Organisering in barnefamilier*, NIBR-Report, 22.

Solberg A. and Vestby, G.M., (1987), *Barns arbeidsliv*, NIBR-Report, 3.

Solberg, A., (1990), "Nagotiating Childhood: Changing Constructions of Age for Norwegian Children", in A. James amd

A. Prout, (eds.), *Constructing and Reconstructing Childhood,* London: Falmer

Solberg, A., (1997), "Negotiating Childhood: Changing Constructions of Age for Norwegian Children", in James, A and Prout, A. (eds.), *Constructing and Reconstructing Childhood,* Second Edition, London: Falmer Press.

Song, M., (1996), "Helping-out: Children's Labour Participation in Chinese Take-Away Businesses in Britain", J. Brannen and M. O'Brien (eds.), *Children in Families,* London: Falmer Press.

Song, M., (1997a), "Children's Labour in Ethnic Family Businesses: The Case of Chinese take-away Busineses in Britain", *Ethnic and Racial Studies,* Vol. 20, No.4, pp. 690-716.

Song, M., (1997b), "You're Becoming more and more English': investigating Chinese Siblings' Cultural Identities", *New Community,* Vol. 23, No. 3, pp. 343-362.

Soni, S.M., Tricker, M. and Ward, R., (1987), "Ethnic Minority Business in Leicester", *Birmingham,* Ashton University.

Speier M., (1982), In c. Jenks (ed), *Sociology of Childhood: Essential Readings,* London: Batsford.

Srinivasan, S., (1995), *The South Asian Petty Bourgeoisie in Britain,* Aldershot: Avebury.

Stanley, L. and Wise, S., (1983), *Breaking out: Feminist consciousness and feminist research,* London: Routledge and Kegan & Paul.

Straus, M.A., (1962), "Work roles and financial responsibility in the socialisation of farm, fringe and town boys", *Rural Sociology,* (27) 257-274.

Saur, D., (1994), "Discrimination Against Girl Child in India", *Social Action,* Vol. 44, July-September, pp. 14-26.

Tatum, C. and Tucker, S., (1998), "The concealed consequences of caring: an examination of the experiences of young carers in the community", *Youth and Policy,* No. 61, Autumn, pp. 12-27

Thomas, N. and O'Kane, C., (1998), "The Ethics of Participatory Research with Children", *Children and Society,* Vol. 12, pp. 336-348.

Thrall, C.A., (1978), "Who does what? Role stereotyping, Children's work and continuity between generations in the household division of labour", *Human Relations,* 31 (March)

Vasant, F., (1991), "Prevailing Conditions of Girl Child", in J.A.

Williams (ed.), *Anatomy of Girl Child*, Madras: Asian Youth Centre.

Wadel, (1979), "The Hidden Work of Everyday Life", in Wallman, S. (ed.), *The Social Anthropology of Work*, London: Academic Press.

Wallman, S., (ed.) (1979), *The Social Anthropology of Work*, London: Academic Press.

Weiner, M., (1991), *The Child and the State in India*, Delhi: Oxford University Press.

Werbner, P., (1990), "Renewing an Industrial Past: British- Pakistani Entrepreneurship in Manchester", *Migration*, Vol. 8, 17-41.

Whitaker, A., (1986), "Child labour and its Causes", *Third World Now*, Spring.

White, B., (1975), The Economic Importance of Children in Javanese Village", in M. Nag (ed.), *Poplation and Social Organisation*, The Hague: Mouton.

White, B., (1982), "Child Labour and Population Growth in Rural Asia", *Development and Change*, Vol. 13, No. 4, pp. 587-610.

White, L.K. and Brinkerhoff, D.B., (1981), "Children's Work in the Family: Its Significance and Meaning", *Journal of Marriage and Family*, Vol. 43, pp. 789-798.

Whiting, B. and Whiting, John W.M., (1975), *Children of six cultures: A Psycho-cultural Analysis*, Cambridge, Mass: Harvard University Press.

Wihstutz, Anne, (2006), "The Significance of Care and Domestic Work to Children: A German Portrayal", in Hungerland *et. al.*, (eds), *Working to be Someone*, London: Jessica Kingsley Publisher

Wilson, P. and Stanworth, J., (1988), "Growth Strategies in Small Asian and Carribean Businesses", *Employment Gazette*, Vol. 96 (1)

Wilson, P., (1983), *Growth Strategies in Minority Enterprise: Case Studies in Corporate Growth of Asian and Afro-Carribean businesses in Britain*, London: Small Business Research Trust.

Winterbottom, M.R., (1958), "The relation of need for achievement to learning experiences in independence and mastery", in J.W. Atkinson (ed.), *Motives in Fantasy, Action and Socity*, Princeton, NJ: Van Nostrand Reinhold.

Wintersberger, (1994), "Costs and Benefits—The Economics of Childhood", in Qvortrup *et. al.*, (ed.), *Childhood Matters*, Aldershot: Avebury.

Wittner J., (1980), "Domestic Labour as work discipline: the Struggle over Housework in Foster Homes", in S.F. Berk (ed.), *Women and Household Labour*, Beverley Hills, CA: Sage.

Woodhead, M., (1998), "Combatting child Labour: listen to what the children say", *Childhood*, Vol. 6, No. 1, pp. 27-49.

Zelizer, V., (1985), *Pricing the Priceless Child*, New York: Basic Book.

Zill, N. and Peterson, J.L., (1982), "Learning to do things without Help", in L.M. Loasa and I.E. Sigel (eds.), *Families as Learning Environments for Children*, NewYork: Plenum Press.

INDEX